Behind the Smile

This book is dedicated to
Reena, Francesca and Ahmed,
three very brave and special children

Behind the Smile

My Story

by LISA POTTS
with JILL WORTH

Hodder & Stoughton
LONDON SYDNEY AUCKLAND

Contents

Foreword

Like almost everybody else I first became aware of Lisa Potts when I saw the horrifying news broadcasts about the attack at St Luke's School on 8 July 1996. At that time I was struck by her courage, her selflessness and her wonderful smile.

I have been lucky enough to meet Lisa on a number of occasions since then and have got to know her better. The more I have learnt of her, the more remarkable she has become. Behind the smile there is a more complex, more human and more interesting person whose qualities as a human being explain why she reacted as she did.

First, anyone reading this account will know that Lisa comes from a strong and united family. It is a story of a young girl growing up with the security and love she needed to flourish.

Second, her love of children started at an early age. Lisa was one of those marvellous children who loved helping out with the little ones and who followed through that early interest in her choice of career.

Third, Lisa is a woman of great courage. Even after meeting her I was still not aware of the extent of the pain and trauma she went through both physically and mentally as a result of the attack. She was a tower of strength to all around her and yet at the same time was suffering dreadfully from the pain and the frustration that disability brings and from flashbacks and nightmares. Truly we had no idea of the agony behind the smile.

Finally and most importantly, Lisa has a strong Christian belief which has helped sustain her throughout her life and particularly during the dark times she experienced after the attack.

Lisa has had to give up working with her beloved children but as everyone reading this book will know she has a great future ahead of her. Whatever her next career, those remarkable qualities of love and courage and caring for others will shine through and bring her great success.

Cherie Booth QC
April 1998

'Smile Lisa!'

'Lisa, can you look up here?'

'Smile over here, Lisa.'

'Down here, Lisa, smile this way!'

'How does it feel to have the George Medal, Lisa?'

How did it feel? At that moment I still couldn't believe it. I was being photographed on the steps of Buckingham Palace, having just been presented with the George Medal – the second highest civilian award for bravery – by Her Majesty the Queen. Ordinary me; ordinary Lisa Potts. I didn't feel any different, except that I was now Lisa Potts GM. And it was for doing something purely instinctive. I just felt so thankful that I reacted as I did on that awful, horrific day in July 1996.

I didn't feel special and I didn't feel a heroine. As I stood there smiling in front of all the photographers, I thought that all the awards I'd been given, even the George Medal, counted as nothing compared to the lives of those little children in the nursery.

PART ONE

BEFORE

1 Early Days

I was born on 4 March 1975 at New Cross Hospital in Wolverhampton – a hospital to which I was to return, in very different circumstances, twenty-one years later. I was Mum and Dad's second baby – my brother, Lee, had been born three years before. Mum brought me home from hospital to my first home in Willenhall. But I only lived there for three years before we moved to the house I've lived in ever since, in Merry Hill, another part of Wolverhampton.

It's strange that one of my first memories is of protecting a child. It was when I was out with my close friend, Clare, who lived near us when we were in Willenhall. She was a year younger than me, and even after I moved to Merry Hill we used to play together. I always thought of her as my little sister. She was smaller than me – she'd even fit into my toy pram so I could wheel her around. I felt very protective of my little Clare and I used to stick up for her. One day her mum, who I called 'Auntie Hazel', took us out butterfly-catching over the fields. It was a lovely day and we were running freely around, enjoying ourselves. Suddenly an angry farmer appeared and shouted at us for being on his land. Clare was frightened, but instead of running to her mum, she ran to hide behind me. She was scared, but she was also giggling, so that made me laugh too. My laughter made the farmer even more mad, which meant he shouted at me more than ever. I've always told Clare that I got into trouble for her.

Clare's been a great friend all my life. When I was seven, she moved to a house in Merry Hill, diagonally opposite our house. We could see each other out of our bedroom windows. The way we played together as children reflected our love of the same things – dolls and dancing. We often got blankets down from our bedrooms and did shows together for hours, charging our families 20p each to come and watch us. Every Saturday we'd wash our dolls' clothes together and hang them on the washing line. I adored dolls. My very first memory is of the day we moved to our new house, around the time of my third birthday, and all I can remember about it is that I'd been given a big doll. Another time, when my brother went to Spain with my auntie and I missed him, Mum bought me a doll – one of those with a squashy body and a solid head. I called her 'Lucy' and I carried her round with me everywhere, telling everyone she was a real baby. Looking back, I suppose my love of dolls and my natural protection of Clare were the starting points of my passion for children.

The beginning of my love for dancing, which soon became a big part of my life, came when I was four, and I started dancing lessons. Dad used to take me to ballet on Saturday mornings, while Mum was working in a bakery, and on Mondays I had tap lessons. I had a strict dancing teacher. I was scared of her, but I liked her once I'd got used to her. I loved to dress up in tutus and swan around at home giving shows to my family. I used to practise in front of the TV, pretending the mantelpiece was the ballet bar, and my brother got really annoyed with me if he was trying to watch football. I'd practise so much in the week so I wouldn't get told off on Saturdays. My teacher called me 'Leeza', pronouncing it with a 'z' instead of an 's'. She was the only one who said my name like that and I used to think it was lovely,

I had a really happy, normal childhood. Lee and I started going to Sunday School at St Joseph's church when we moved to Merry Hill. Mum took us; Dad only went at Christmas and Easter, until about four years ago, when he started going regularly. One of my Sunday School teachers there, Pam, was going to become very important to me in later years. Before long I started calling her 'Auntie Pam', and eventually called her 'Mummy Two'. The vicar, Mr Jack, came to visit me lots of times when I was five and had to stay in hospital for a month. I was seriously ill with a virus, following measles, and every time Mr Jack visited he brought a new *Mr Man* book. I had so many visitors. I was in a bed next to a tiny baby, and I used to lie there and look at her for ages. I felt very sad when the baby was moved to another hospital. Mum brought me a black doll and I called her 'Tawaya', after Dr Tawaya, one of the black doctors. I adored that doll.

I was discharged after a month in hospital, and Dad's sister Auntie Jen came with Mum to collect me. When I got home, Dad had just finished hoovering and he was putting the hoover away. I didn't know it then, but sixteen years later, the next time I came out of New Cross Hospital, I would remember that moment, because Dad would be doing exactly the same thing when I got back to the house. He had a thing about cleaning the house at weekends, although Mum did it the rest of the week.

When I came out of hospital I didn't want to go back to sleeping alone, so we got bunk beds and I moved into Lee's room. Lee wanted the top one, so I slept at the bottom. We used to have great fun, playing at shipwrecks – if we fell off the bunks, the sharks would get us. My life was full of imagination. I used to make up games with dolls and teddies for hours on end. Clare and I played at home with Lee and Clare's brother Carl, or with two girls from church, Amanda and Nicola. We often played schools with some other girls who lived over the road. I always had to be the teacher, and I'd set them sums – even though I hated doing them myself. Clare was really my best 'home' friend, but my best friend from school, once I started infants, was Rebecca. One day Rebecca and I even cut our fingers and rubbed the blood together, vowing to be blood sisters for ever and ever. When we were six years old her mum remarried and Rebecca and I were bridesmaids.

Rebecca was always cleverer than me at school. I was a middle-of-the-road child, appalling at maths, but good at English. When I had a month off school because of being in hospital, I had to start having extra lessons. We went to Warstones Primary School, which was near our house. I don't remember anything about the nursery, except that the toilets were very small. Then when I was in Reception, I leaned over the wall and kissed a boy called Charles on the cheek. He left the school after that – I don't think it was anything to do with my kiss – and I had another boyfriend called Shannon. He had blond hair and big blue eyes and we used to play ice-cream vans together. He was older than me, and when he went up to Juniors before me I was upset.

I loved school and I'll never forget the teachers. All through my school days I always liked teachers who were strict but kind – similar to Dad. Mrs Fabian was my first teacher, then Mrs Lewins. After that it was Mrs Wood and I really loved her. She was so kind and gentle and she liked me. In the last Infants class I had Mrs Squire, who was really kind and knew how much I struggled with maths. In the first year of Juniors I had my ultimate favourite teacher, Miss Green. She drove a TR7 and was sporty-looking. She was strict but she loved us. If we were really good we got to help her clean up the room. She told Mum that I had the ability to do well, and I'd be helped by the fact that my group of friends were bright. One day when it was raining I thought I was going to be late and I started crying. When I got into the classroom she comforted me: 'It's all right, Lisa, don't worry.' I remember thinking that one day I wanted to be like Miss Green.

When Clare came to live over the road she started going to my school. In the mornings her mum, Auntie Hazel, took us, and my mum collected us in the afternoons. My brother went alone – he was three years older and thought he was too big to have an adult with him. Every afternoon Mum was there to meet us without fail. She'd either bring a Fudge bar or she'd take us across the road to the Star shop and we'd get ten pence-worth of penny sweets. Sometimes there were other children as well as Clare and me, but Mum would make sure there was something for all of them, although we weren't exactly rich. One day it was snowing and the school heating had stopped working, so parents were contacted to collect the children early. Mum was working, so Dad came to collect us. We went home in the car instead of walking, and he made us some soup. I thought it was really exciting.

Dad could be great fun. Every Christmas he dressed up as Santa and made the downstairs loo into his grotto. Mum rang bells to say that Santa was coming, and my friends used to come and visit him. I believed in Father Christmas, even when Lee and my cousin Dawn told me there was no such person. I was terribly upset because I knew that there was. But the year I was seven, I realised they were right. On Christmas Eve, I saw my dad riding a bike across the garden from Auntie Hazel's, where it had been hidden. He was putting it in our shed, ready to give to me the next morning. It was supposed to have been my present from Santa.

Christmas at home was always so happy. On Christmas Eve, Mum always gave us new pyjamas to wear. They were thick and Christmassy, sometimes red tartan. Then we'd leave out carrots and a bowl of water for the reindeer, and whisky for Father Christmas. I couldn't work out why Clare left him Cinzano instead. We didn't discover for years that it was because my mum liked whisky, and Clare's mum liked Cinzano.

Lee and I woke up very early on Christmas morning to empty our stockings. At about five o'clock, I'd lean out of my window and call across the street, 'Clare, has Father Christmas been to your house?' Then at half past six we'd go down to open our presents. The house was full of presents, which I always arranged in piles – Mum's, Dad's, Lee's and mine. Dad didn't open his until after dinner. In the morning he'd be there with a black dustbin bag, picking up the paper we'd strewn around. Later on Mum, Lee and I went to church while Dad cooked the dinner. After dinner Lee and I played with our toys, then we'd sometimes have visitors, such as Nan, Mum's mother, or we'd go to visit other members of the family.

Nan lived on the other side of town. She used to come over every Monday morning before school and she always brought us presents. She made us cheese on toast for breakfast, and sat on a stool in the corner of the kitchen. My grandad had died before I was born. My other grandma, Dad's mother, died when I was seven, and Dad's father died when I was nine. We used to go over to see him on Saturdays, and have tongue sandwiches and Fisherman's Friends. I always ate mine off a silver plate. He lived in a high-rise flat, and I loved to look out of the window and find our house. Grandad had had a stroke and so he used to bang with his stick and shout when he wanted anything. Grandad was an even louder character than Dad – and he's pretty loud. Dad shouts when he's talking, and one girl who came to our house for tea was so scared of him that she wanted to go home. I used to wonder why he had to talk so loud when he's such a gentle giant really.

I felt so secure in the routine of our lives. Every Friday night Mum went shopping while Lee and I watched *Crackerjack*. It was great fun when she came home and we could eat what she'd bought. On Sundays Mum cooked the dinner and Dad went to the pub, but he was always back in time for dinner. I'd wolf it down so Lee and I could go out to play. Lee and his friend Mike used to set up Olympics for the children in our road. They made medals and charts and stood us on boxes to give us our medals. Lee and I had baths together on Sunday nights when we were really young, then sat by the fire and watched television. We went to bed when we were tired. Mum and Dad were never strict about bedtimes and we always knew when we were ready for bed. Mum would come upstairs to tuck us in, and to have a talk and a kiss. For years I said the same thing as she left the room: 'Don't switch the light off, don't shut the door, till Daddy gets up in the morning.'

On Saturday nights, Mum, Dad, Lee and I went to the Club for a family night out. All the children did disco dancing, which was great fun. Clare came too, and Emma, the daughter of one of Dad's friends from work. We used to go on holiday with Emma's family. They were great holidays. Dad panicked when we were packing to go, worrying about being late and fitting things in the car, but then we'd stop for petrol and comics and everything was all right again. The first of those holidays was at a guest house in St Ives. One night Mum dressed Emma and me as Hawaiian girls for the fancy dress and we won a huge bar of chocolate each. We went straight upstairs and ate the whole lot. Mum always made wonderful costumes and hats and I used to win the competitions at the Sunday School Christmas parties as well. Emma had a little sister, Katie, who was born when we were about eight. We played Mums constantly with her, until she was about four years old. She used to follow us around, but by then we were eleven or twelve and were going through a phase where we thought we were grown up, so we didn't want her.

My family had a saying: 'Wherever there's an accident, Lisa will be there.' I was accident-prone – one of those children who has to keep being rushed off to Accident and Emergency. I was always falling over, and I broke my arm twice, once by doing a forward roll at Junior school and again by falling off the back of a chair. Another time a big piece of plaster fell off the ceiling. Of course, I had to be the one sitting right underneath. Once a keyboard which we kept on top of a wardrobe fell on my head when I opened the wardrobe door, and I had to stay in hospital overnight. I loved Ovaltine, and one day I climbed up onto the kitchen worktop to reach the cupboard where it was kept. I had two spoonfuls, but after I'd put the jar away, I decided I wanted more. But this time when I opened the cupboard, I cut my eye on the corner of the door and had to go to hospital for stitches. Another day, when our neighbour was gardening, I asked if I could go round to help. As I stepped out of our gateway I was knocked over by a bike and had to have stitches again. Perhaps all these were practice runs for the day I'd need stitches and Accident and Emergency in a big way.

I was also scared of dogs. I remember one day in particular, when a huge Alsatian dog got into our garden. I was petrified. I screamed and screamed, then just ran into the house. I liked cats, though, although I was allergic to them. One day when I was nine, Dad went to get the lawnmower from the shed and a stray cat ran out. We went in and found four baby kittens. Mum doesn't like cats, so we couldn't have them in the house, but we looked after them in the shed. Eventually the mother cat went away. The Olympics were on, and we set up hurdles for our version in the garden. The black cat won all the races – we called him 'Ed Moses' after the Olympic runner. Then Clare took one kitten, and two went to Auntie Jen's friends. Mum overcame her fear and we were able to keep the remaining one. Three months later, I came home from tap dancing to find Lee crying in the bedroom. The cat had been run over. I didn't cry then, but I got upset later at Brownies. Only the week before, Clare's cat had been run over too.

I was an easy-going child, but I used to worry I'd get things wrong. The school had a system of sad faces and happy faces, and I was worried about getting sad faces, even though I only got a couple all the way through the school. I wasn't confident when it came to anything academic, especially maths, but if I was doing anything that involved dancing or mothering I was much more confident. I loved English and drama, but my favourite lessons were dancing and singing. I'd always be in the Infants and Junior plays, and I'd get good parts – usually dancing roles – in the Christmas plays. In the third year of Junior school I did a solo tap dance in *Cinderella*, and in the final year I had a main dancing part in the summer play. I was also chosen to play the title role in *Annie* with an amateur dramatics company at the local theatre. By then I had a most fantastic dance teacher at school, Miss Prosser, who always chose me in PE and games. It always thrilled me to be chosen for something. It was the same with Brownies. I'd been going to Brownies every Monday evening from the age of seven, and when I was ten I was promoted to a Sixer. I thought only clever girls were chosen, so I felt really proud when I got my two stripes as Sixer of the Elves. I enjoyed Brownies. We went on pack holiday every year, but I really missed Mum. Then I used to find she'd put chocolate and biscuits in my case, and I'd lie in the church hall and pass them along to everyone. We did shows for the leaders at the end of the pack holidays and I always thought I knew all about it and ought to organise it.

When it was time to pick a Secondary school, I chose St Peter's Church of England School. Looking back, it was an unusual choice for me to make, because I wasn't going with my friends. My brother went to another school, Smestow, but that didn't influence me. Lee and I had always been good friends, and a close bond would grow between us in the future, but at that stage the three-year gap in our ages made a difference. Lee was always reading books, making games out of cardboard, or playing the computer in his room. We weren't sharing a bedroom any more and, although he'd let me go in to see him for five or ten minutes, he'd soon say it was time for me to go back to my room. I'd leave my door open, though, so that when his friends came round I could see them come up the stairs and call hello. So I didn't feel I needed to follow Lee to Smestow, even though some of my friends were going there too. Most of my friends were going to Highfields School, but I thought Highfields was too big, and I was only one of a few from our Junior school to choose St Peter's. I don't know now why I made that choice, except that I liked the school when I went to visit, and I liked the uniform.

When it came to the last day at Junior school, though, I felt very upset to be leaving my friends, particularly Rebecca. But that summer was very busy with shopping for my new uniform and lots of rehearsals. At the end of my last year of Junior school I'd been chosen to play one of the coolie dancers in *The Mikado* at the Central Youth Theatre. The director, Chas Rimmer, had held auditions and only three of us who were auditioned from our school got parts, so I was very excited. The dress rehearsal for *The Mikado* was the night before I was due to start Senior school. Dad was supposed to pick me up, but it finished early and I had a lift home with someone else. I was so worried about Dad – would he know I'd left early? I was anxious about him until he arrived home. I was the same with Lee. He used to go to football on Saturday afternoons, and when it was time for him to arrive home, I used to stand outside and wait. I was worried if he was ten minutes late, thinking he'd got hurt.

I don't remember being at all stressed or worried by the fact that the performance of *The Mikado* coincided with the first days at Secondary school. I just knew I wanted to be in it, and it was fantastic. I suppose by the time I started St Peter's I thought I'd become an adult. At eleven, Clare seemed so young compared to me. She was a tomboy and she still played with dolls, whereas I was by then growing up and putting dolls away. Even so, our friendship didn't fade away – I still looked on her as my 'little sister' – and the following year Clare joined me at St Peter's.

I liked the school and made new friends. One was Andrea who was really strong, and I used to hide behind her. It was a bit of a role reversal from the way it had been with Clare. The adolescent years were starting, and I was very conscious of myself and my weight. I wasn't fat – you could probably describe me as 'chunky'. That good feeling I had when I was praised hadn't left me, and in one art lesson the teacher asked us to copy the painting of Van Gogh's *Sunflowers*. I'd never been good at art, but I thought it was such a pretty picture – and of my favourite flowers too – so I tried hard. He looked at my painting, and said, 'That's really beautiful.' It was the first time I'd been praised in art and it felt so good. It brought tears to my eyes and the memory has stayed with me to this day.

By the end of the second year I'd become really interested in children and I loved seeing babies. Mum had started taking a Sunday School class, and I used to help her. Together we planned the stories and did the artwork. I loved it, and absolutely adored the children. I was thirteen and I loved being with six-year-olds. So, at the start of the third year, the run-up to choosing options for GCSE, I was disappointed to find there was no childcare course at St Peter's. I wasn't all that happy at school by then, and I told Mum I wanted to move to Smestow. Mum had always let me make my own choices. She never pushed me into anything, but just said, 'Are you sure you really want to? It's up to you.' She'd been like that when I chose to take part in *The Mikado*, even though it clashed with the start of Secondary school, and she'd let me choose to go to St Peter's when I was eleven. Now she was giving me the choice again. I left St Peter's that Christmas and started at my new school in January 1989.

2 A New School

I fitted in straight away at Smestow. I met up with my old friends and made lots of new friends too. Suddenly my early adolescent awkwardness was disappearing; I became popular and less self-conscious. I also got thinner and started to be much more aware of trend and fashion. The only problem I had at first was that the teachers assumed I was much cleverer than I was. Lee, who had just gone into the sixth form at Smestow, was very clever, so everyone thought I'd take after my brother. I was put into all the top groups. I tried to tell them I couldn't cope, and in maths I was eventually put down from group one to group four. In the other subjects I remained average throughout the rest of my school days.

For the three years I was at the school, my form tutor was Mr Caine, a bald-headed man with glasses, who was the kindest teacher at the school. He had so much enthusiasm for everything, and for all of us. I took notice of that, and I flowered, flourished and glowed. I'd been continuing with my acting and dancing; I had been chosen to play the Artful Dodger in *Oliver*, and went back to the Central Youth Theatre for *West Side Story*. When we did *West Side Story* again, this time at school, I danced a duet, for which I choreographed the whole dance. I felt so proud of it.

It was when I started at Smestow that a bond was formed between me and my brother. He was sixteen and I was thirteen and we became very close. We walked to school together, talking about anything and everything. For part of the journey we played a game about the passing cars – we each had to say what jobs we thought the drivers had. Then I'd quite often ask him if I was getting it right in class. I never felt stressed by not being like Lee. I suppose I knew I was never going to be clever from the day I was born. I loved going to Smestow and liked my work, but life was a laugh, and I didn't take things too seriously then.

I started to be a bit of a joker. Before the teacher came in to take the lesson, I'd stand up and sing songs from *Annie*, then quickly sit down when the teacher arrived. Everyone thought I was a nutter, but I think they liked it. I don't think I annoyed them. I'd watch films and then imitate the actors, taking on all the parts. It was my way of expressing myself. I don't think I was hiding behind all those roles I took on. My real personality was cheeky and funny, and playing the fool just made me funnier.

I was learning to express myself, and there was nothing I liked more than to talk to my friends. At dinner times we went down to the field and talked about which boys were good-looking. Maths was still my big problem, but I'd talk about clothes and fashion in the lessons. We'd turn our chairs round and pretend to work, but really we just wrote the date and then waved to people in the classroom opposite. I was never naughty in other lessons – except for writing notes to my friends – and I always did my work and handed it in. I was cheeky, but in a funny way, never nasty. I wanted to be friends with everyone, and never wanted to hurt anyone's feelings.

My favourite lesson was English, and when we read books like *Of Mice and Men* or *To Kill a Mockingbird*, I'd put my hand up to read every part. I wanted to do all the different voices. I still enjoyed running, PE and games. Again, I was average, but I really enjoyed it. It got all my energy out. I never tried to get out of PE, and I loved the showers afterwards. Most people rushed through, clutching their towels, but I stood there and washed my hair, singing. Then came another of those times when I was praised for something. I'd choreographed a dance which four of us were going to perform for Open Day. We practised every dinner time. Mrs Walker, another strict but kind teacher who was head of PE, watched us practise, and afterwards she said, 'That was fantastic, all of you. And well done, Lisa, for bringing it all together.' It made me realise that I really was quite good, and that warm feeling you get when you're praised has stayed with me ever since. It boosted my confidence, but I never felt big-headed, just pleased that I could do something. I'm sure that all those words of praise I received at different times during my school life had a positive effect on my character. It shows what a difference praise makes to a child – and what an influence teachers can have too.

I was fourteen that March, and several things happened which marked the fact that I was growing up. Some friends of my parents asked me to babysit for their three children. I started to go over there every Saturday night and they became like a second family to me. John, the father, picked me up, and sometimes I'd chat to Michelle in her bedroom while she was getting ready. Other times I'd give the children their tea, or I'd clear up. I used to bath the two youngest children, Samantha and Dean, who were five and three, then we'd play downstairs with their toys. Looking back now, I can see I was still a child at fourteen, but I felt so grown up at the time. After the children had gone to bed, I felt the house was mine for the night. I loved cleaning the house, even though I never liked cleaning at home. They had beautiful bathrooms, and a gym in the garage, which I was allowed to use. It was wonderful.

A few weeks after that, I started going out with Adam, my first real boyfriend, who lived opposite me. On 1 May 1989, a bank holiday, I invited him round to our house, and he asked me out then. I'd just turned fourteen, and he was nearly sixteen. I'd wave to him from the kitchen window while I was making breakfast every morning. We were to spend a lot of time together over the next two years. I'd moved on from Brownies to Guides, and I enjoyed it, but after I started seeing Adam, I left. I felt too grown up for it, although I kept going to church and to Pathfinders, a youth group, as well as helping Mum with her Sunday School class. I decided I wanted to be confirmed. Lee and I had been christened together and now we went to confirmation classes together. We were the youngest ones in the group.

At about this time I was travelling on the top deck of a bus on the way home from a friend's house. As soon as I sat down I noticed that three boys on the back row were bullying a Down's syndrome boy who was sitting across the aisle parallel to me. They were throwing bits of paper at him and calling him horrible names. I didn't do anything about it at first, but after a minute I couldn't stand them being so cruel. I was scared to death – they were about eighteen years old – but I felt so sad for the boy that I had to do something. I turned round and said, 'What's he ever done to you? Why can't you leave him alone?' The lads looked at me and one of them said, 'Who do you think you're talking to?' Then he got up and started to come towards me. The Down's syndrome boy was crying, and he said this was his bus stop, so I grabbed his hand to take him downstairs and kicked the lad who had walked up to us. I told the bus driver there were lads upstairs picking on this boy, then we got off the bus together. The boy was crying and all he said was, 'Thank you.' He must have known where I lived, because a couple of days later he came to my house and put a letter through the door saying, 'Thank you for helping me.'

When I went back to school that September, I was starting my GCSE courses. We all had to do maths, a science (I took biology), French, English language and literature. We could choose our other subjects, so I picked typing, history and, of course, childcare. It felt so good to be doing the childcare course. It was my favourite subject, the best lesson ever. English was easily beaten into second place. I took childcare seriously – this is where I was going, and I just knew I was going to be a nursery nurse or a teacher. Because I knew that, I wanted to work really hard at it, and I went out of my way to be the best in the class. In the other lessons I still wrote notes to friends and sometimes messed about, even when I enjoyed the lesson. In fact, my typing teacher said, 'Lisa is good at typing but she can't sit still. She always has to be dancing around.' But in childcare I was never like that. I really concentrated and did even more work than I was asked to.

At the start of that term I stopped going to my Saturday dancing lessons. I'd been going for ten years, and I wasn't sad to leave. Like Guides, I felt I'd grown out of it. Instead, I started my first Saturday job in a clothes shop. It was so badly paid – I got £9 a day, yet I was getting £15 for babysitting on Saturday nights! Soon after that I got a job in W H Smiths' record department in the run-up to Christmas. Dancing was too much in my blood for me to give it up for long, though. Six months after leaving the classes, I enrolled at another school of dance which was more relaxed. This time I did it for fun, not seriously. While I

21

was there, I was chosen to be a model, and I started modelling hair and clothes. Once I modelled bridesmaids' dresses at the Dome in Birmingham. Adam came to watch my dancing shows now, which was so embarrassing. Friends from school came too, and they'd always whistle and shout at me. Mum, as usual, was there every night, and she sent me flowers or a teddy bear to the stage door, as she always did. It made me feel so special, particularly when I heard the call, 'Lisa Potts to stage door.'

On Friday nights and Saturday, if I wasn't babysitting, Adam and I went with his friends to Bantock Park, a large field and playground, where young people used to hang out at the weekend. We were in love, and we'd walk up there hand in hand. The lads played football, but I wasn't into hanging around. Our friends laughed at me because I was always rushing off somewhere to do other things. They also said I was posh because Mum had always dressed me in smart clothes, although the girls were only too keen to borrow my clothes when they wanted to look smart themselves! But now I didn't want to be dressed up all the time. One girl said to me, 'Why don't you ever wear a track suit?' I wanted to have one, so Dad took me out and bought me a green and white one.

Soon after that we started going to the pub. I didn't drink – I didn't like the taste of alcohol then, and I was too young anyway – but I used to buy a soft drink and keep filling up the empty glass with water from the sink in the Ladies. When I was fifteen I went to a night club for the first time and I remember feeling really young to be going there. I easily passed for eighteen. My parents always knew where I was and I phoned to tell them if I was going to be late, so I was never in trouble with them. But I took them for granted – they were always there for me, they fed and watered me, and kissed me when I went to bed. I didn't realise until I was older how much they cared for me and worried about me. Fortunately, they liked Adam – he was so polite and he always took care of me. But I worried about him in the same way that I worried about Dad and Lee when I was younger. I wanted him in my sight all the time.

In October 1990 Lee went to university and Mum cried for weeks. Suddenly it was like being an only child. Lee wasn't there to mess about with, and I couldn't talk to him at bedtime in one of our rooms. It was hard to adjust. I still had Adam, Clare and many other friends, but it wasn't the same. The year Lee left home was my fifth year at school, and we had to do work experience. I decided I wanted to go into a Primary school. With my friend Vicky, who also loved children, I went to my old Infants school, Warstones. It was fantastic. I simply loved it. I worked with Mrs Astley in the Reception class. I wanted to be so helpful and did anything she wanted me to do. Mrs Astley wrote me a glowing report, suggesting I became a teacher rather than a nursery nurse. I read that report over and over again – she really thought I was good enough to be a teacher! Vicky also got a good report and I was proud of her too. Again, someone had praised me above the average and it made me feel so good.

I took my mock GCSEs at the beginning of the spring term and passed seven. I didn't pass maths, of course. I decided I didn't need to do much work after that, which turned out to be a mistake, as I discovered when I got the results of the real exams and I'd only passed four. Fortunately, I didn't need to do any better to get a place on the nursery nurse course I'd decided to take when I left school. I'd applied for Nursery Nurse Examination Board (NNEB) courses at four colleges and was offered a place at every one. The college I wanted was Walsall College of

Art and Technology, and in April the letter arrived to say I'd got a place. I was still in bed when Mum came up with the post. I was so excited when I read the letter, and Mum put her arms round me and said, 'Well done!' She always praised me to the highest height. I got as much praise from her as Lee did. Vicky accepted a place at one of the other colleges, and for hours we discussed the nursery we were going to open together one day. We made plans about how we'd set it up and what we'd call it. My mind was quite made up – I was going to work with children, as a nursery nurse and, who knows, maybe even as a teacher.

When it came to the last day of school, in June 1991, I was sad. I was particularly upset that I'd no longer see the teachers. Everyone wrote over each other's shirt and we were hugging and crying. But on the way home I thought, 'I'm in the bigger world now.' This was going to be the start of 'my new career'. By that time, Adam and I had split up. It was on 5 May, two years and four days since we'd first gone out together. His mum had remarried and moved to Leicester, and after a while he went to live with her. I just couldn't believe it at first. Neither of us wanted it to end, but we decided that because we were so young it was better to finish than to keep trying to visit each other when we lived so far apart. Every day I cried, and every day we wrote to each other. I missed him so much. But at the time I was about to start my GCSE exams, so I had something to occupy me, and I feel as if I became independent then.

That summer I was busy working with Michelle's children, and I had another baby to care for. When I was fifteen, my cousin Dawn, who is five years older than me, had a baby, Ashley. If I looked on Clare as my little sister, then I looked on Dawn as my older sister, and I loved to babysit for Dawn and her husband Terry. When Ashley was asleep in his cot I was worried about him because I couldn't hear him breathe. I'd rock him to wake him up, then when he cried, I'd walk around the room with him, pretending he was mine. I loved him. I also became very close to Dawn, and in a few years' time I was to be at the birth of her second baby – which was one of the best days of that year.

3 My First Job

My GCSE results arrived in the post when Mum was on holiday with Auntie Pam. It didn't worry me at all to find I'd only passed four with grades A-C: English literature, English language, history and childcare. In fact, I was really happy about it. I'd never expected to get eight like Lee. When I told Mum, she was as happy as I was. And when term started at Walsall College in September, I knew this was the life I wanted. I went straight into my first work placement, Little London Primary School in Willenhall. I worked in the Nursery and Reception classes with three- to five-year-olds for two weeks. The nursery nurse there, Jane Rafferty, was the best I worked with in all my work placements. I learnt so much from her. She taught me small but important things, such as when the children showed me a painting, I shouldn't say, 'That's nice, what is it?' but, 'Tell me about it'; and she showed me how to make better displays of the children's art. I never felt criticised – it was all part of learning.

After two weeks I went into the college, and the term continued with one week on placement at Little London and one week in college. It was the start of masses of assignments – education, health, art and craft, computers, professionalism, first-aid, and so on. I loved it so much. I was so interested in it all. It took over an hour to get to college. I had to leave home at quarter to eight, and didn't get home until about 6.30. I soon made new friends, particularly another student, Danielle. And on the very first day at college, I met a girl called Nici on the bus. We just started talking, and from then on we sat together every day and became great friends. She wasn't a student; we left each other in Wolverhampton, where I caught a second bus to college and she went to work. She became yet another one I worried about – when she wasn't on the bus, I'd wonder what was wrong.

On Fridays college was only open from 9 a.m. to 11 a.m., and it seemed such a long journey just for that. So every other Friday, instead of going to college, I went shopping in Birmingham. I'd take the £10 I'd earned from babysitting on Thursday nights and would often spend it on clothes. I used to copy up all the work, so I didn't miss out. It didn't take so long to get to my placement at Little London School and, although I could leave there at 3.30, I always stayed later. I never went shopping on the Fridays I was on placement. Those days were far too important and I hated missing them, even when I was ill.

When I was going out with Adam, we went round in a group with his friends. I'd carried on seeing them after Adam left and had become very friendly with another of the lads, Marc. I'd gone shopping with Marc on Saturdays for about a year – even when I was still going out with Adam – and we'd developed a good brother–sister relationship. In November Marc asked me out and from then on love blossomed. He was gorgeous – it's strange that I never used to see him in that way before. He'd changed from a brother figure to a man I was to be involved with for the next five years. And throughout those five years we were as much best friends as we were romantically attached.

Marc's personality was totally different from mine. He was more laid back and gentle, with a loving way about him. He was quiet while I was talkative – I probably drowned him out! I felt so proud that I was going out with him. He was eighteen and I was sixteen – although I felt as if I was eighteen. Marc was so supportive throughout college. I'd go to his house after college and work there. He helped me with art, and found things out for me to put in my anthology of work. Looking back, I feel that Adam was my school love, while Marc was the start of adulthood.

I worked on placement at Little London school for two terms, and was sorry to leave the following Easter. I really enjoyed doing my observations – watching an individual child's emotional skills, language, social skills, and so on. After the Easter holidays Danielle and I started a one-term placement at a Social Services Day Nursery which was very different. The children had come in with problems; some had been abused or had severe behavioural problems. I took a great interest in them and loved doing observations on these children, particularly looking at how their social skills developed, compared to children brought up in a more normal setting.

In March Auntie Pam's mother, Nanny Teece, had died. Pam had been close to our family since we met her at St Joseph's Sunday School when I was three. Now she was to become closer to us than ever. Nanny Teece had been housebound and Pam had lived with her. I'd loved going to visit them from when I was a little child. They lived in one of the first houses to be built on the estate, and Nanny Teece often talked to me about how she used to look out on fields when she first moved in. Once, when I had to do a history project on the local area, she helped me so much and I got a high mark. I made a tape of her talking and drew a map of the way it used to look around her house.

I'd bought her two china rabbits for Easter and she'd put them on her windowsill, saying it would be like looking out at the rabbits in the field, as she used to. On the day of her funeral, the rabbits were there on the windowsill. Auntie Pam already had her own key to our house and, now she lived alone, she came to us even more. She became one of the family, usually eating with us and sometimes staying for weekends and going on holiday with Mum and Dad. From then on, if Auntie Pam wasn't at home when I came in from college, I'd miss her.

In May two exciting things happened. I went on holiday to America for two weeks with Michelle and John, to help look after the children. They'd asked me a few weeks before, but it meant taking time out of college and I was so nervous about asking. My friend Danielle told me to just ask, but I panicked, and couldn't. In the end Michelle wrote a letter, explaining that I'd be getting lots of experience of childcare while I was away, and that it was only for one week of college time, as the other week fell in half-term. When I eventually found the nerve to ask Mrs Glazzard, the course principal, she just said, 'Yes, do go, and have a lovely time.' I wondered why I'd made such a fuss. I was so excited to be able to go. We stayed in a villa, and I wasn't treated as their nanny but as one of the family. My 'work' was doing the ironing, making the children's tea, playing with them in the massive pool – and going to Disneyland and Universal Studios. I did miss Marc, though, and we phoned each other every day.

The other thing that happened that month was that I became a Brownie leader. I'd left Guides when I was fourteen, but that May the Brown Owl from my own childhood Brownie days asked Mum if I'd like to be a leader. I was most touched by this and said I'd love to. The children had to choose my name and they chose Sunny

Owl. They said it was because I had blonde hair and was really silly and laughing all the time. It was a rush to get to Brownies straight after college on Mondays, but I adored being there. I loved the games evenings and helping the children with the dancing and jester badges. I started to go on pack holidays and in the summer I was warranted as a Guider by the Commissioner.

When term started again after the summer, there seemed to be even more work to do, but it never got me down. I loved getting up in the morning, even with the long haul to college. My first placement that year was with a Year One class at Allumwell School. It was a grand class, but I didn't enjoy it as much as Nursery and Reception. I love that three-to-five age group. But I learnt a lot. I helped with the Christmas play the staff put on for the children. I played Rapunzel, and that's what the children called me afterwards. Each placement was different, and my next one, in January, was as a nanny for triplets, who were about eight months old. Their mum was really nice, and so organised – the children had had baths and breakfast before I got there. She'd got her budget sorted out and did lots of cooking on Mondays to freeze it for the week. Then one terrible day, one of the little girls was crying constantly and we couldn't find out why. We took her to hospital, and they found her arm had been pulled out of its socket. I was so afraid that I might have done it while I was playing with her. Her mum said that even if it was me, it wasn't my fault, and I hadn't meant to do it, but I was terribly upset. The little girl had her arm put straight back into its socket at the hospital and her mum phoned me that evening to tell me she was playing happily. I felt so relieved.

I'd been taking driving lessons since my seventeenth birthday and had taken my test the previous November, but I failed. I took it again in February 1993, the month before my eighteenth birthday, and passed that time. My parents bought me a Y-registration white Metro for my birthday. It came from our next-door neighbours and cost £200, so I put something towards it too. On the night of my eighteenth, in March, I went to a night club with my friends. I expected to feel 'Yeah, I'm eighteen!' – but I was disappointed. It was boring; I'd done it all before.

In my last term I spent two weeks at Walsall Manor Hospital. For the first week I was on the baby ward, which was lovely. I couldn't pick the babies up very often, but I used to touch them when their mums weren't there. I loved the smell, and I used to stroke them and smell them. For the second week I was on the children's ward, where I kept the children occupied and happy, played games and encouraged them to do paintings. That was good fun. For my final placement I went into different schools with a speech therapist, seeing many children with special needs. Then it was time for exams. Whereas at school I was petrified when it came to exams, at college I was confident, because I knew what I was doing and I was so interested. College had meant two years of hard work, but one thing I'll always remember is that I did well because I put so much effort into it, and loved it.

One of the saddest things about leaving college after exams was that I wouldn't see Nici on the bus every morning, but we made arrangements to go out together once a week, and she is now one of my best friends. I went to the pub with my college friends on the last day of college, and the very next day I started work as a part-time nanny for Michelle who was about six months pregnant. While I was nannying, I stayed at my cousin Dawn's, if her husband was on nights. By this time Ashley was four years old and great fun to play with. Dawn and I stayed up late chatting, even though I had to get up at 6.30 to be at

Michelle's for seven o'clock. I gave her children their breakfast and took them to school in the car – college had finished, but the schools were still open. The children laughed at my old banger. I loved those children. I'd watched them grow up since I was fourteen. I spent the summer holidays with them, going for walks, playing and doing housework. When Marc had time off work he came with me to Michelle's. He loved children too. In September, Michelle had her fourth baby, Cassie. But by then I'd been offered a job at a private day nursery, Tiggywinkles.

I'd been applying for jobs since before I left college and would have liked to work in a school, but most schools like their applicants to have experience. I was so nervous at the interview – this might actually be *my* job. The nursery was in a big old converted house, and the first room was the baby room, the second room was for toddlers, and upstairs was the three-to-five unit. I fell in love with the place and with all the children. I was told that they had some other people to interview and they'd let me know. When I finally got the letter to say I could start in two weeks' time, in the toddler room, I was so excited. I jumped up and down, hugging Mum.

When I started the job I was given my uniform, a long blue skirt and a red polo shirt saying 'Tiggywinkles Day Nursery'. I instantly loved all the staff. There were nine members of staff altogether. Marie was a fantastic nursery nurse who'd been there for about four years, and I liked to watch her and think, 'That's how I want to be.' She gave out so much patience and love. In my breaks, I loved to sit and chat with the cleaner, Linda, and the cook, Anne (I called her Annabella). I worked shifts of 8 a.m. to 4 p.m. or 10 a.m. to 6 p.m. All the children and staff ate dinner together and I usually had a baby to feed. We just had half-an-hour break before or after dinner. I had to clean the toilets after dinner, so they'd be ready for the afternoon children coming in. The toddlers were still in nappies, so I helped with potty-training. It was lovely to start to train them and a month or so later see them come in wearing pants. We used to have a conveyer belt of about twenty nappies to change. It took a long time because, after all, they were children and I wanted to chat to them and blow raspberries on their tummies. Most of them would be crying, so I'd sing nursery rhymes as loud as I could to drown the noise. It usually stopped the crying. It was long hours for not much pay, but I loved it.

The toddler room was bright and cheerful, and I enjoyed helping to introduce new ideas and set up different activities. I liked the toddler age group, but I really wanted to get my hands on the threes-to-fives. I dropped hints that I'd like to move upstairs, and after six months they moved me up. All the children were adorable, and I got on well with the parents too. The play was more structured and I used to plan things at home in the evenings. Since starting work, I'd missed doing my college work in the evenings, so it was good to get back to something that involved preparation. Even so, after a year in the job, I decided I wanted to do something more. I really wanted to get into education. Although I cried a lot when I left, and missed all the staff, I knew it was the best thing for me. They gave me a grand send-off, with a huge banner saying, 'We will miss you, Lisa.' The children sang for me and I had so many presents and cards.

I'd been applying for jobs in schools, but I hadn't got them. I knew I needed experience before I could be offered a job, so it was a vicious circle – I couldn't get the experience until I'd got the job; I couldn't get the job until I'd got the experience. Then Auntie Pam, who was Deputy Head at St Luke's Junior School, suggested I should apply to do voluntary work at St Luke's Infants School. She gave me the phone number and, very nervously, I rang Denise Bennett, the Head Teacher of St Luke's Infants, who asked me to go in to see her. I was so frightened, but she made me feel welcome. I visited all the classes and the teachers welcomed me too. By the end of the day it had been arranged that I would start work there, voluntarily, in September. I'd found my way into a school! But little did I know that I would leave St Luke's so sadly, two years later.

I began my voluntary work at St Luke's at the beginning of September. Auntie Pam gave me a lift as far as St Luke's Junior School, then I had a five-minute walk past some blocks of flats to get to the Infants School. In one of those flats lived a man called Horrett Campbell – but of course I'd never heard of him then.

4 Happy Days at St Luke's

There wasn't a nursery at St Luke's when I started, so I worked mainly in Reception and Year One. I listened to the children reading, did art and craft, and was on a storytime rota for different classrooms. During that autumn term, Denise talked a lot about opening a nursery and, of course, I thought, 'Oh, she'll need a nursery nurse!' At the end of term she took me into an empty classroom next to the Reception class. It was used as a storeroom, or for sewing, and sometimes there was an English-speaking class for Asian mums in there. Denise said to me, 'This is where we'll have the nursery,' but I didn't believe it would happen.

I'd kept on sending out my CV and applying for jobs while I was at St Luke's. I eventually got an interview for a mornings-only nursery nurse post at Dawley Brook School. It was to cover maternity leave, so it would only last from January to April, but I was thrilled to be offered the post – my first paid job in a school. Apart from anything else, it was good to be earning again after several months of voluntary work. I'd got used to earning money while I was at the day nursery, and I'd managed to save enough to go on two holidays that year – to Ibiza with Clare and the Algarve with Marc. I started working with a

Year One class at Dawley Brook in January 1995. It was a long day. I left home at 7.30 a.m. and worked at Dawley Brook from 8.30 to 12.00. I ate lunch on the bus on the way to St Luke's, where I was continuing with my voluntary work in the afternoons. I arrived there at 1.20, just as the bell was ringing for the start of afternoon school. Mondays were even more crazy – I had a staff meeting at St Luke's straight after school, then rushed home for tea, out again to Brownies and on to aerobics. I got home at quarter to ten, then Clare came round for a cup of hot chocolate and a chat.

I gained so much confidence while I was at Dawley Brook. The teacher gave me groups of children to work with, and treated me as if I had lots to offer. She taught me so much and I tried to do as much as I could for her. She was full of good ideas. While I was there we changed the home corner into a vet's surgery, a doctor's surgery and a space ship. I watched her doing her plans for English, maths, technology and all the other subjects. I was never really good at the different subjects – just good at being with children. My work at St Luke's changed that term too. Instead of working in the classrooms every afternoon, Denise asked me if I'd like to start sorting out some of the junk in the room she wanted to use as a nursery. So it looked as if this nursery really could open after all. I felt as if I was working towards something and remember feeling a great sense of achievement when I'd finished clearing and washing a set of twelve drawers and their contents. I washed the toys that we'd want to keep and labelled everything. It was great fun, but for the first few weeks there was no sign of the nursery happening.

Then in February, Denise started to make real plans. The nursery would open soon after Easter. One day I was sitting in the office with Denise and Pam Shee, the school secretary, ordering the equipment we'd need, when Denise suddenly asked if I'd like to apply for the job of temporary nursery nurse. I wouldn't need an interview, but because I was working there voluntarily anyway, I could take it on until August 31st. I was over the moon. I'd been offered a full-time job in education and I was only nineteen! My job at Dawley Brook finished that Easter, which meant another sad leaving day, but I knew I was moving on to my first full-time job in a school. I had lots of presents and a bouquet of flowers at my farewell, and the children put on a lovely assembly for me.

There was still so much to do to get the nursery ready, but before we started the serious work, I had an important experience which I now believe was God preparing me for what was to come in sixteen months' time. Jackie, one of the Brownie leaders, asked me to go with her to a church in town. It was a lively service, with people dancing and speaking in tongues. I wasn't frightened, but I felt as if it was another world. At the end, people were asked to go to the front for prayer. Hands were laid on them and they started falling backwards. I thought they couldn't really be falling backwards like that – someone must be pushing them. Jackie asked me if I'd like to go up. I hesitated at first, but then I did. The pastor laid his hands on my head and all at once my whole body felt like a raging fire, and I could feel myself falling. I don't know how long I lay on the floor, but when I came round, Jackie was kneeling beside me. I cried for nearly an hour afterwards. When I went home I told Mum and Auntie Pam what had happened, and Pam gave me a book to read about this sort of spiritual experience. Since then I've read my Bible every day. I used to pray every night, but now I began to talk to God as a friend at any time of the day or night. I also became less selfish and more understanding of other people's needs. I started going with Jackie to her church every Sunday night, while still running the crèche at my own church, St Joseph's, on Sunday mornings.

During the Easter holidays Denise and I, with Carol, a teacher who was on maternity leave, went into the school nearly every day, cleaning, disinfecting, filling skips, painting and knocking in nails. The toilets and doors were changed to make them more suitable for small children and the tiles for the surface of the playground were laid. It was so exciting to see the dumping ground becoming a nursery. It was due to open at the beginning of May, two weeks after the start of the summer term. Those first two weeks of term were complete madness, but so exciting and such a challenge. I just loved to get up in the mornings. I made picture labels for the coat hooks and signs saying things like 'This is the nursery' and 'Please wash your hands'. We put backing paper on the display boards for the children's work to go on, and swept out the boiler shed so we could keep the bikes in there. Dorothy Hawes, the teacher I'd be working with in the nursery, listened to my ideas when we organised the timetable. Occasionally I went with the teachers to do home visits to the children who would be coming into the nursery, but most of the time I was in the middle of getting it all done. The carpet wasn't laid until four days before we opened. Kit, another nursery nurse, had made fantastic beanbags to match the ladybird theme on the curtains. When it was all ready, I stood at the very end of the room, looking at this gorgeous, bright nursery. It was a lovely feeling. I wished I'd taken photographs all the way through the transformation. I stood back and thought, 'It's all ready. After the weekend comes the big day.'

And, boy, did that big day come! Dorothy and I got in early to prepare everything – dough play, jigsaws, sand,

Me, aged 20 months, and my brother, Lee, aged four and a half, 1976

The 1st Merry Hill Brownies where I am Sunny Owl

With Marc on holiday in America

St Luke's nursery where I worked

The aftermath of the Teddy Bears' Picnic

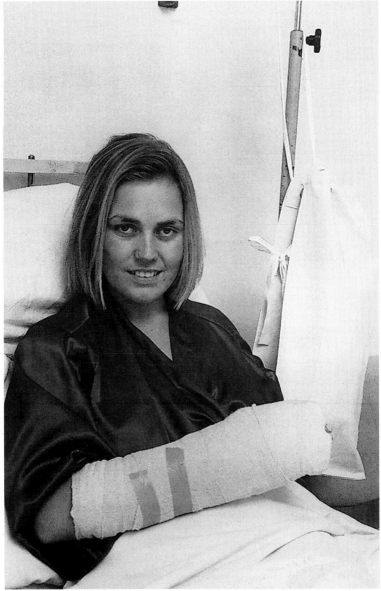

In New Cross Hospital with my arms in splints

A week after the attack with the toys that were sent to me

Police find Horrett Campbell in the
Villiers House flats in Wolverhampton

Home from hospital surrounded by cards, flowers and gifts

Convalescing in my garden at home

Mum, Dad, Lee and myself

My first meeting with Ahmed after the attack,
with his sister, Marium

water, cars, colouring, sticking and gluing, dressing up, book corner – there was so much going on. We'd arranged a staggered intake, with children coming in at nine o'clock and 9.30. The parents stayed for a while, then gradually left. Then it was just me, Dorothy and eighteen children. Gosh – I don't know how I had the patience. At one point there were ten children crying and I was singing 'Oh how I love to be at nursery' at the top of my voice. I think Dorothy thought she was going to be working with a nutcase. We just couldn't calm them down. For many of them it was the first day they'd been left by themselves. We stopped for a drink and an apple. That was funny – there were three apples, and I'm no good at maths, so I just sliced them at random. Some pieces were thin and others were huge. After the first day, Dorothy cut the apples.

When the children arrived for the afternoon nursery the whole process started again. Most of them were crying, but we kept our spirits high. As the days went on, it got easier. After three weeks there were only one or two who cried, and they were mainly children who didn't have English as their first language.

It was a good term. I built up a relationship with Dorothy, who had worked at St Luke's for over twenty years. She already knew most of the parents, many of whom had older children at the school. Although Dorothy was the teacher and I was the nursery nurse, she didn't give me all the dirty work. She shared jobs like cleaning the toilets and gave me the chance of doing some of the educational work. I admired Dorothy's dedication to her work. We could leave at quarter to four, and I often stayed until 4.30, but Dorothy would sometimes still be there at six o'clock. I'd come in the next day and find she'd put up beautiful work on the display boards.

During that term, 'my' job had to be advertised. I applied, but I didn't assume I'd get it. The others would probably have more experience than I'd had. On the afternoon of the interviews Kath, another nursery nurse, took my place in the nursery while I went to wait in the staff-room with the other three applicants. They didn't look nervous, but I was terrified – even though I knew the people who were going to interview me! My neck went red, which it always does when I'm nervous, and all I could think was that I was going to be sick. My heart was racing when I was called in. There were four people on the panel – Mark Jones, the curate of St Luke's, Mr Fallon, the chair of the governors, his wife, who's also a governor, and Denise. I don't remember all the questions they asked me, or what I said. I do know they didn't ask me about what you do when a man rushes at children with a machete. I remember just one question, which was about how to teach music to the class. All this jargon flowed out of my mouth and I thought, 'Am I talking rubbish?' All the time crazy thoughts were going through my head: 'I need to get back to the children to say goodbye, they're going home at 3.15. I'm going to be sick and I'll make a mess on the carpet. But this is *my* job – I may never see the children again after this term if I don't perform well at the interview.' I couldn't think of anything except these mixed-up thoughts, but all the time I was still answering their questions.

Then it was back to the staff-room to wait. Eventually Denise came in and said, 'Thank you all for coming, but Lisa Potts, would you like to come with me, you've got the post.' When I went back into the interview room, they all said, 'Well done,' and all I could say was 'Thank you.' And there I was with a full-time contract. It was the following day before my red neck went back to its normal colour.

Dorothy gave me a Forever Friends teddy bear and a congratulations card saying 'Looking forward to working with you next term'. We started to plan for the next term, together with Nicola, a new nursery nurse who was going to start work in September in both the nursery and Reception class, and another teacher, Dorothy Clulow. Nicola had been a year above me at college and it was good to know I was going to be working with someone around my age. Almost immediately Nicola and I got on well together, and we soon became good friends out of work hours too. At the end of term, Dorothy Hawes gave me another card saying how much she'd enjoyed working with me. And then it was summer holiday 1995, with a full-time job to look forward to at the end of it.

I enjoyed that summer. Auntie Pam, who was retiring on health grounds, bought a new car on 1 August, so she was selling her K-registration Nova. She said I could buy it from her, and she'd give me £1,000 towards it – an advance twenty-first birthday present. I arranged a bank loan which I'd pay back monthly. So on 1 August, aged only twenty, I drove away in her Nova. I still cherish that car. Marc had passed his test two months before and he'd bought a Polo, so I was really excited. I said goodbye to my old Metro, which had started to let me down. The previous Christmas Eve I'd gone out to collect Dad from the pub, wearing my pyjamas, dressing-gown and Garfield slippers, when the Metro broke down. I had to get out and push it down the road. A man stopped to help me and I kept apologising to him for wearing Garfield slippers. About three months later I met him while I was out one evening and was so embarrassed when he said, 'Nice to see you with your clothes on.' So it was good to get a reliable car.

It wasn't only getting the car that made that summer so

good. Marc and I went on holiday to Aberystwyth, and I went to visit Lee in Nottingham. He'd finished his degree at Sheffield, and was now doing a PhD. I started to build a good relationship with his girlfriend, Helen. I also went to a converted farmhouse in Oswestry with our youth leader from church to visit a Church Pastoral Aid Society camp for deprived children – I was going to be a leader there the following year. I started going to aerobics three times a week, twice locally and once with Marc's mum. Marc lived with his dad about five minutes' walk from me, and his mum lived in Telford, but we spent a lot of time with her. I'd been doing aerobics twice a week since the previous January, and in the summer I changed it to three times because I wanted to lose weight. I'd started having a weight problem while I was at college – I'd stopped dancing, and I was sitting down much of the time. That summer holidays I met a girl I used to dance with, Louise, and she persuaded me to start dancing again, but I said I'd only do it when I'd lost another stone. I still babysat for Michelle's children and for Ashley, and saw lots of friends, so the summer passed all too quickly.

Not that I wasn't happy when it was time to start my job at St Luke's, though. Soon after term started we had the official opening of the nursery. All the staff and children watched Mr Fallon, the Chair of governors, cut the ribbon in front of the nursery and declare it open. Some of the children who had been in the nursery the previous term had started Infants, but most were the same. Because we had only a few new ones, there wasn't so much crying. I felt much more confident. I'd found my feet and I knew what I was doing. The two Dorothys, Nicola and I made a good team. One of my favourite things was taking the children down to the hall for PE, even though it took nearly all the time to get there and back. We taught them to line up and walk down to the hall and we helped them take off their shoes and socks. We only had about twenty minutes of PE before it was time to put on their socks, do up laces and buckles and line them up again for the walk back to the nursery. But it was all part of the learning process.

I loved to dress them up in the home corner too. Reena, a little girl who wouldn't speak, played happily at dressing up with some of the other children. Once she spoke to them, and when she realised I'd heard, she glanced up at me shyly and went completely quiet again. Francesca was another quiet one – she was so adorable and sweet. She'd whisper, 'Hello Miss Potts,' and if anyone pulled her hair she wouldn't say who it was, or stick up for herself, she'd just say 'Someone pulled my hair' in a small voice. Another girl, Marium, had very little English, but I watched her blossom into a real chatterer. I loved them all to bits. One day when Marium was being collected from school she introduced me to Ahmed, her little brother, who was nearly three. He was too young for nursery then, but was going to start the following September. He would come for his introductory visit to the nursery in July – and after that day, it was a miracle he was still alive to start nursery at all.

Towards the end of term we had the Ofsted inspectors in, so there was quite a stressful build-up to their visit. On the day they were in the nursery I burnt the Christmas biscuits I was making with the children. I was in a panic, wondering if this would mean bad marks. Nicola and I were wafting the air with tea towels, trying to make the smell go away. But when the report arrived, the nursery had been highly praised.

That Christmas was lovely. I think I look back on it as being good because the next one was so horrible. I went to the Christingle service on Christmas Eve, then over to

Dawn's, and back for midnight mass. On Christmas morning Marc came round at nine o'clock and Auntie Pam arrived a bit later. I still arranged the presents in piles for each person, and we all watched each other opening them one at a time. Then Marc went to his dad's for lunch and I phoned Ashley, then went over to Clare's to see what she'd had for Christmas. After lunch we watched the Queen's speech, Lee and I washed up, then I went with Marc to have tea with his mum. It was a traditional Christmas, but it holds such good memories.

On New Year's Eve Marc and I went out with Dawn and Terry for dinner, then back to their flat, where we finally fell asleep at four in the morning. Dawn, who was desperate for another baby, told me that night that she was sure she was pregnant, but two weeks later she found she wasn't. I felt so sad for her. Little did I think on New Year's Eve that the following year was going to turn my life upside down. I thought I'd carry on as usual for years, working in the nursery, and I couldn't imagine Marc and I ever splitting up. But I didn't know anything about what was to come, so I began the new term in January with as much enjoyment as usual. I loved every minute of being with the children, learnt new things and had new ideas. Now I was down to my ideal weight of nine-and-a-half stone I started dancing again. My dancing teacher welcomed me back. I still went out every Thursday night with Nici, who I'd met on the bus the first day at college. So with all that, plus aerobics, Brownies, running the Sunday morning crèche, seeing Dawn, Clare, Marc and lots of other friends, life was good.

I was so full of enthusiasm about the nursery. We needed to raise some more money and I had the idea of starting dancing classes in school. I began that January with six children from Year Two. They paid 50p each and stayed for an hour after school. They loved it, so it was worthwhile, although some people asked me why I bothered for only six children. Then I decided to run an aerobics class for the staff. They paid £1 each session and used to complain that I was wearing them out. I told them it was doing them good. Sometimes I'd get seven of them, so with their money, plus the money from the children's dancing classes, I could raise as much as £10 a week for the school. I became so fit with those classes, as well as the aerobics and dancing I was doing out of school, and I was eating healthily. God had prepared me spiritually for what was to come and, looking back, I believe he was preparing me physically as well.

In March I celebrated my twenty-first birthday with Mum, Dad, Lee, Pam and Marc. We went to a Greek restaurant; Dad bought a bottle of champagne and Mum and Pam had taken flowers and a cake to the restaurant earlier in the day. The cake was brought out, complete with candles, and everyone sang 'Happy Birthday'. A few weeks later I went on pack holiday with the Brownies – four days away on airbeds in a church hall. It was great fun – long walks, dancing and story-telling. Three of the leaders put on a show for the children. I was both Snow White and the Wicked Queen, which was quite a feat, and the other two were all of the dwarfs. The children were in stitches – they must have thought what fools we were making of ourselves as we rushed around the stage trying to be too many people at once. I told them bedtime stories, acting out all the different voices, and they roared with laughter, but it didn't make them go to sleep. I was the first-aider. I always was, because I'd taken a certificate at college. I loved pack holidays, and I loved the children.

Towards the end of the summer term, Dorothy decided we'd invite all the children who were due to start in

September to the nursery for a teddy bears' picnic. Our theme that term was brown – we chose a different colour every term – so we'd do things like making jacket potatoes and brown dough. Brown teddy bears fitted the theme perfectly. It so happened that the whole of the Infants was having a teddy bears' picnic, but Dorothy didn't want the nursery to be involved with that, partly because she thought it would be overwhelming for the little children. So, a week before we were due to have ours, all the Reception, Year One and Year Two children went down to the field for their picnic. Denise had agreed to it, but I felt sad, because all our nursery children were looking out of the window at the others and asking when it would be their turn for the picnic.

Their turn would come the following Monday. Who could possibly have dreamt that such a dreadful thing was going to happen to interrupt it? I made individual invitations with every child, which they addressed to their parents: 'We are going to have a teddy bears' picnic on July 8th. We are going to bring our teddy bears. You are invited too.' I helped make forty-four of these, and on Friday 5 July they all went home clutching their invitations.

I was on good form that weekend. I was a youth leader at a Christian camp, along with our church youth worker, Mike, and two others from church, Shirley and Steve. I worked with the seven- to ten-year-olds and bonded with them really well. It was a mixture of Christian teaching and other activities – including aerobics, of course! On the Saturday night I played Sandy in a performance of extracts from *Grease*. After I'd done a song and dance I said in jest, 'One of these days I'm going to be so famous' – not knowing that three days later my name would be on the front page of all the newspapers. Three days later, when

Steve came to visit me in hospital, he reminded me of what I'd said.

On the way home I was telling the others all about the teddy bears' picnic we were having the following day. Later that evening I went round to Marc's. I was as happy as usual. I told him all about the weekend, and when I left him that night I said, 'See you on Tuesday – I love you very much.' What seems strange is that I can remember the small details of that night so clearly – what we were wearing, what we said. Perhaps that's because the following day I wouldn't be Lisa Potts the happy-go-lucky nursery nurse any more. The events of the next day would scar me and change my whole life for ever.

PART TWO

THE ATTACK

MONDAY 8 JULY 1996

5 A Teddy Bears' Picnic

When I woke up in the morning, it was just like any other day. I rushed around, ate breakfast and chatted to my mum. I'll never forget the kiss and hug I gave Mum when I left that morning. At the time it felt just like the hug and kiss I usually gave her. It was only after the attack that it stuck out in my memory. It could have been the last kiss I ever gave her.

I drove off to school with my teddy sitting on the passenger seat next to me. When I arrived at school, Dorothy was blowing up balloons and had started preparing the picnic. I began to help, getting the face paints ready because we were going to make all the children look like teddy bears. Dorothy had been hard at work making teddy bear sandwiches, and she had brought chocolates, tablecloths, napkins and badges, all with teddy bears on them.

There were two picnics that day, one for the morning children and another for the afternoon children. Mum and Pam came to help with the morning picnic, as well as some of the mums. We all had a wonderful time, especially the children, who left with their balloons, painted faces and their teddies and chocolates. Mum and Pam went home, as Mum had to go to work, and as I said goodbye I said I'd see them later on. Monday was my busiest day, with a staff meeting, Brownies and aerobics. Then Dorothy and I prepared all the picnic things again, ready for the afternoon children. I blew up more balloons, cleaned the toilets and prepared the face paints, then went off for my lunch with Nicola.

I was wearing a long black pleated skirt, a white linen shirt and a dark red cardigan and burgundy loafers. It was fairly warm that day, so I remember taking my cardigan off before I went back into the nursery. The children were so excited that afternoon as they ran in with their teddy bears under their arms. I remember little Francesca coming in looking as beautiful as ever; she came up to me and said, 'Miss Potts, do you like my pretty dress?' I said, 'Francesca, you're looking very beautiful today.' She smiled and ran off to find her name to stick on the board, as the children did every day when they arrived. Then Marium ran in shouting, 'I've brought my brother Ahmed today.' Her little brother appeared behind her, smiling. This was his first visit to the nursery, a taster visit to see what it was going to be like, before he started the next September. Ahmed didn't speak much English, so Marium did most of the talking for him. His mum came up to me and asked, 'Will he be all right?' I assured her that he would have a great time. That short sentence will never leave my mind. Soon I would be carrying around the guilt that this little boy was going to be scarred for the rest of his life.

Some of the mums came to help that afternoon too. Reena's mum, Surinder, was there, as well as Fatama's mum. Two others brought their two-year-old sons: Emma Parlor's mum Philippa and her son Ben, and Teresa's mum, who was nine months pregnant, and her son Dominic. A lady called Sheila had also come in; she was thinking of doing nursery nurse training and had phoned Denise to ask if she could come in to gain some experience. I made her a cup of tea and showed her round when she arrived. The children were so excited as we painted their faces and played different party games with their teddies inside the nursery. Francesca and Reena wanted to be pandas, so I gave them white faces. One little boy, Taishion, said he didn't want a teddy bear face, so I suggested he just had a nose and whiskers and he agreed to that. Taishion said to me, 'Your teddy bear's nice, Miss Potts.' It was a lovely teddy Dorothy had bought me the previous Christmas. The children were fascinated by it – it snored and its tummy went up and down when it lay on its back, and it laughed when it was thrown into the air. I told Taishion he could play with it if he wanted and he went off happily, clutching my teddy.

When it was time to go outside and have the picnic, Dorothy, the mothers and I started to sit the children down around the tablecloth with their teddies on their laps. We passed round the sandwiches, crisps, teddy bear biscuits and chocolates. While the children were happily tucking in, I went inside to make drinks for the parents. As I went in, I looked through the glass in the nursery door which led into the Reception class and saw Linda, the temporary Reception teacher, busy leaning over one of the children, showing him how to do something. I walked over to the other side of the nursery to make the drinks, and saw Nakita's mum standing in the doorway. 'Come on in – all the children are having their picnic,' I said to her. We started to chat, then I took the drinks out to the mums, who were standing against the nursery fence. We talked about the lovely weather and I said, 'Only a week left of term and then you'll have the children under your feet for six weeks.' They were all laughing.

It was such a happy, relaxed atmosphere. Emma's mum,

Philippa, said, 'Let's have a photo of you, Miss Potts.' I asked her to wait while I took my hair-band off. I hated my hair being pulled back from my face, and had only put it in a ponytail so it didn't get in the way while I was working with the children. Philippa took a photo of me cuddling her daughter Emma, who was laughing because I was hugging her big Garfield cat at the same time. I went back in to get the rest of the drinks and saw two other mums just coming in to the nursery. I offered them a drink too, and we were joking about me not being able to make tea very well. They said they were just going out of the school gates to have a cigarette, and left me saying, 'We won't be long, see you in a minute.' I looked at my watch and saw it was a couple of minutes past three o'clock.

It had become a little dull so I went in to put my cardigan back on. Back outside, some of the children came running up to hug me and hold my hand. Nakita asked me to go to the field with them, and the children pulled me onto the the small grass area where we started to play Ring-o-ring-a-roses with their teddy bears. There were about eight children with me; the rest were playing on the soft play area with the skipping ropes and balls.

Dorothy called over to me to ask the time, as she never wears a watch. I said, 'Gosh, it's 3.12,' and remember thinking how quickly the time had gone. Dorothy called, 'Come on then, children, time to pack away now. Put the balls and skipping ropes in the basket and then line up against the wall.' Some of the children went to line up against the wall straight away and others were still running around on the grass. I started to collect up the skipping ropes and balls with some of the children, then I bent down and was showing Francesca how to fold the ropes up properly so they wouldn't get in a knot.

I heard Dorothy say, 'Hello, how are you?' I turned

round to see that she was speaking to Wendy Willington, one of the mums who was walking on the Infants field, the other side of the three-foot fence, on her way to pick up her son from the Infants school. I said, 'Hello,' and as I turned back round again I saw, out of the corner of my eye, a man running round the side of the school building. He was tall and black and he was wearing a trilby hat. A grey bag was slung across his chest and in his right hand he was carrying a large knife. It looked like a plastic toy because it had no shine on it. I heard Dorothy say, 'Quick, run inside,' and she shepherded some of the children into the nursery. In another second the man had lifted the knife above his head and smashed it straight down on Wendy's head. I saw her carrier bag fall to the ground, then she fell too. There was blood everywhere, and at that point I knew it was no plastic knife.

Suddenly there was complete chaos and panic. The children were screaming, the parents were screaming, but somehow I felt very calm. I grabbed some of the children in my arms and turned to run. As I spun round, I saw the man bring the knife down on Reena's mum's head. Surinder half-turned as if to run, then collapsed. Then he did the same to Fatama's mum. I felt my long skirt rise up as children gathered underneath it, screaming my name. The man leapt across the fence; his lips were drawn back and there was the most frightening, angry grimace on his face. It was as if he was laughing. I ran with the children towards the nursery door, pushing and shoving them inside. I saw Dorothy about ten feet inside the nursery, and re-member thinking she had a lot of the children with her, but there must be some left outside, so I knew I had to go back. That was the last I saw of Dorothy until she came to visit me later in hospital.

As I turned to run back outside for more children, the

man's face was right up against mine. I lifted both my hands to shield my face and watched this huge blade strike down into my left arm. I didn't feel any pain, just a feeling of wetness on my cardigan. I didn't know then that he had cut my hand and arm half off, and that underneath my red cardigan, my hand was hanging loose.

I started grabbing some of the children and pushing them inside. The man lifted the knife to strike Francesca, who was holding on to my skirt. It looked as if he was going for her neck, and I flung out my left hand to protect her. It lasted a fraction of a second – the knife started to descend, my hand went up, the knife skimmed above my hand and straight across her face. The whole of her left cheek was ripped apart. I looked into her eyes – they were totally glazed. I couldn't believe what was happening. This couldn't be real. No-one would do this to innocent children.

The man turned round and was waving his knife in the air and running around. I didn't see Francesca again, but I found out later that she'd somehow managed to get into the Reception classroom with the teacher Linda. I ran with a couple more children to the nursery door and pushed them inside, then spun round again and saw Marium and Ahmed were still outside. For a fraction of a second I thought, 'What am I going to do? Shall I go inside with the other children, or get Marium and Ahmed?' I knew immediately there was no way I could leave the two of them outside. As I ran back, Marium ran full force into me, screaming, 'My brother, my brother!' Ahmed was running after her, with the man chasing them both. Then Ahmed fell. The man was right behind him, with the knife raised. I ran to pick Ahmed up, although I have no idea to this day how I lifted him when my hand was hanging loose. It has to be a miracle. But even as I picked him up, the man sliced across his head. I put my right hand in the way, but the same slice that cut Ahmed's head open also ripped open my hand. I saw a lot of blood everywhere, and Ahmed became very quiet.

I made it inside with the children and tried to pull the door shut. But it wouldn't shut. I looked down and saw the man's foot was in the doorway. The door to the Reception class was to the side of me. We could run through there and into the main school building. The man was right behind me as I reached out to open the Reception class door, but as I tried to turn the handle, I suddenly knew I couldn't go that way. There were about twenty-five children in the Reception classroom and all their lives would be in danger if I opened the door and the man followed us in. What I didn't know then was that Linda was holding the door shut on the other side. She knew she had to protect the children who were in her class, but it must have been so hard for her to make the decision to hold the door shut against me. Afterwards she told me how she saw the man raise his knife against me on the other side of the door, and she said, 'My own daughters are about your age, and it was just like having to watch one of them being attacked.'

Too late, I realised we should have gone the other way. We should have run straight through the nursery. We were going to be trapped. I was in a very small area with the man behind me, the closed Reception door in front of me, a dressing-up trolley on one side and some cupboards the other side. To run round the corner and through into the nursery, the man would have to move – and I couldn't exactly ask him to do that. There were about six or seven children trapped with me. One of them was Reena, staring at me with her face sliced open. All the children were screaming and I was frantic. I knew there was no way I would be able to get them all out alive. I had to protect them, and I had to think fast.

I put Ahmed down on the floor at the side of the dressing-up area where he could be hidden with clothes. The only way the other children would survive was if I gathered them all in front of me, protected by my body. I bent over them and put my arms around them. As I leaned over their huddled little bodies, the man brought the machete down twice on my back. I thank God so much that I felt no pain, just pure adrenalin running through me. The children were shouting, 'Miss Potts!' I will never forget their piercing screams. They will stay with me for the rest of my life. I was sure I was going to die, and I'll never know why the man decided to turn and go back out of the door into the playground again, but he did.

As soon as I realised he was going, I began to kick and push the children around the corner, so they could run through the nursery and out of the far door into the school's main entrance. I knew Ahmed was still at the side of the dressing-up area and there were feet sticking out of the dressing-up trolley, but I had to leave them there so that I could take the other children to safety. I knew they'd be safe enough there – he wouldn't see them. Marium was clinging to my dress, still screaming for her brother, Reena was under one of my arms and another child under the other. I was weighed down with children clinging to my skirt and I pushed them to make them run in front of me.

As I started to run I felt a blow go down the back of my head. The man had turned back; he hadn't gone out into the playground after all. It was the only pain I felt and it was a very quick and sharp pain, but I carried on running with the children under my arms. Right in front of us, blocking our way, was a big water tray. I thought the man was chasing me – I had to get over it somehow, and I mustn't drop the children. I took one great leap and landed on the other side. I will never know how I jumped over such a huge object, especially with the two children under my arms and such severe injuries to my hands. It seems too fantastic to be true; all I know is that we made it.

When I got to the other side of the nursery I turned, expecting the man to be there, but he had gone. I didn't see him again until I had to face him in court five months later. In that quick backward glance I saw all the beautiful colours of the nursery. It's a sight I'll never forget. The nursery was never the same place to me again.

I ran out of the door at the other end of the nursery, which leads out to the school's main entrance. People were screaming and shouting, 'Where's the man?' I could see Denise at the school entrance and I dropped the children in front of her. Pam Shee, the secretary, took them from me, and Denise pushed me inside the main school building, saying, 'Oh no, Lisa.' Dorothy Clulow took me through the dining hall where parents and children were screaming at the sight of me. I wondered why, until I looked down and saw that I was leaving a river of blood behind me. Blood was pouring down my face and from all over my body. Nicola appeared and led me away from other people into the activity area, where it would be quieter, and Dorothy ran to get a towel. Nicola asked, 'Lisa, what's happened to you?' I realised she had no idea about the attack. She and Dorothy Clulow had been working with a group of children in the dining hall that afternoon. It seemed so strange that the four classes at the far end of the school were still busy at work. I thought they surely must know because the attack had gone on for such a long time – but then I realised it had probably lasted for no more than one and a half minutes. My voice was so calm as I answered Nicola: 'A man jumped the fence and attacked me and some of the children with a machete.' I don't know how I knew the knife was called a machete – I wasn't aware I even knew what a machete was.

Dorothy Clulow returned with the towel and Nicola wrapped it round my arm, while Kath, the other nursery nurse, was trying to mop up the blood as it poured from me. Standing near me was Sarah Poole, who was to be the new Reception teacher in September. She had come to visit the school for the day, and I tried to joke with her, 'What a day to visit!' but nobody seemed to find it funny. I felt so calm, but looking back now I can see I was in total shock. It was as if I was in another world from everyone else. I thought I must be in the middle of a nightmare and I was going to wake up.

I asked Nicola if I could see my arm. She lifted my cardigan and I saw the worst sight I've ever seen. My hand and lower arm were nearly hanging off and I could see bone sticking out. It looked like a lump of meat hanging in an abattoir. Kath asked Nicola to wrap the towel round me again and I asked her if she'd hold it very tightly. I thought I was going to bleed to death before the ambulance arrived. I reached round to my back and felt inside it and then felt my head. It was as if I needed to touch my wounds. I said, 'I'm bleeding from everywhere.' My cardigan was covered in hair, as if I'd been to the hairdresser's and the hair was itching on my neck.

I heard the school bell ring. It was set to go off at 3.20, and I was amazed to realise it could only have been eight minutes since the attack began. A teacher who was in the classroom opposite opened the door to let her children out. She said, 'Lisa, what have you done?' Kath quickly asked her to keep the children inside the classroom for a moment. All of a sudden one of the mothers ran in screaming, 'This man's got a gun, he's going to kill us all!'

and she ran through to get her child from one of the classrooms. I said to Nicola, quite calmly, 'I don't think he has. I didn't see a gun.' At the same time I thought, 'I've survived all this and if he's come back with a gun there's no way any of us are going to survive.'

At that point two policemen came running through the door. One said to me, 'Are you all right?' and I said, 'Yes, I'm fine.' He held up a grey bag in front of me and said, 'Do you know if this is his?' I just answered, 'Yes.' The next moment I felt a huge sense of relief because Nicola told me the ambulance had arrived. She led me to the door, with the deafening screaming and crying echoing in my ears. Standing in the doorway was Ahmed's mum, with Marium screaming by her side, and Ahmed in her arms. Ahmed's head was hanging down and his eyes were shut. I thought he was dead and that I was to blame. I said to his mum, 'I'm sorry, I did all I could.' She smiled at me and said in a shaky voice, 'Are you all right, Miss Potts?' I smiled at her and carried on walking. I was lost and trapped in my own world. Here I was walking to the ambulance when children were dead – or so I believed at the time.

One of the ambulance men asked if I wanted a stretcher and I said, 'No, I can walk.' I couldn't let the children see me being carried out on a stretcher – they would think I was dead. I was determined to walk to that ambulance all by myself. The walk from the door to the ambulance is a complete blur now, but the next thing I remember is Nicola helping me up the step of the ambulance. She wanted to come to hospital with me, but there was no room. 'You'll be all right,' she said, as she handed me through the door, but her face was so pale and she didn't look very hopeful. I look back now and think how hard it must have been for Nicola to see her friend covered in blood and completely quiet, when she knew what a chatterbox I usually was. As she left the ambulance she gave me a half-smile. I wondered if I would ever see her again, let alone everyone else, especially my family and Marc. But these thoughts were swept away because in front of me two ambulance men were lifting Francesca off the bed so I could lie there instead. It was the first time I had seen Francesca since she was attacked in the playground. She was in a complete daze and a paramedic was trying to deal with her cut, which was gaping open from her mouth to her ear. She lifted her head slightly and, gazing at me with her huge eyes, mouthed, 'Miss Potts.' Those two words meant everything to me. To hear your own name being spoken by a child who is in such pain is so moving. All I wanted to do was reach out and love her, but I couldn't.

Reena's mum, Surinder, was sitting at the other side of the ambulance, with Reena on her lap. Reena was screaming constantly and her mum, who had also been hit, just sat in complete shock. The paramedic who dealt with me was very calm but I knew that inside he must be in a terrible state of shock to have been called out to the scene of such a horrendous attack. He asked my name and I told him in a voice which was as calm as his. He began to attend to my back and head and to stem the flow of blood, which seemed to be coming from everywhere, while his colleague was dealing with Francesca. I wondered why we couldn't leave, then realised it was because children need a parent or guardian to travel with them in an ambulance. No-one could find Francesca's grandmother, who lived nearby and met her from school. I heard them calling outside, 'Mrs Quintyne!' Then suddenly I heard her screaming Francesca's name. The next minute a policeman handed her into the ambulance, and through the opened doors I glimpsed people still screaming and running around. Denise appeared at the doors and said, 'You're going to be all right, aren't you?' But then someone shouted, 'Let's go!' and the doors were slammed shut.

The paramedic said, 'Lisa, I'm going to have to cut your cardigan off,' and he started to cut the buttons and then the sleeve. I said to him, 'You can't do that – this cardigan is from Next.' He smiled at me and said, 'I'm sure you'll get another one.' When I look back now I think how typical it was of me that when my arm was hanging off, I was more worried about my cardigan. But much more serious than that was the children. I told the paramedic I couldn't leave the school until all the children were out of the nursery and I hadn't told anyone about the children in the dressing-up box. Would anyone know they were there? He reassured me that someone would be taking care of them.

The four-mile journey seemed to last only a few seconds in one way, but in another, the agony of seeing those precious children in so much pain made it seem like a lifetime. I remember seeing the insole of my shoe stuck under my arm – a bizarre sight, as I had absolutely no idea how it could have got there. I lay back as I was told, although I didn't want to because I thought I'd pass out. The noise of the siren which accompanied us on our way is a sound that still scares me now whenever I hear it. Francesca's grandma was screaming and so was Reena. I have a vague memory of trying to console the children and tell them that we would be at hospital soon. It wasn't until a few weeks later that Simon, the policeman who drove the ambulance, told my mum that I was chatting to the children as if there was nothing wrong with me. Apparently I was telling them that we would go into hospital to get some special plasters and these would make us so much better that we would be back at school in no time. At that point I had no idea what an effect this ordeal was going to have on the rest of my life.

Then we stopped and the doors were flung open at the Accident and Emergency department of New Cross Hospital. The staff were ready and waiting and as I was being wheeled in I thought, 'This is just like *Casualty*.' A pretty nurse was half-running next to me, asking my name and telling me what was going to happen. She was only about my age and throughout the next couple of hours she remained calm and professional. As we rushed down a long corridor my main feeling was that I hated the mask on my face because for the first time in my life I was prevented from speaking. Then I was lifted from the stretcher onto a bed. I didn't feel any pain and I didn't feel like crying – until I looked through the gap in the curtains. Right opposite me was Francesca. She was lying so still; I could see her little face and I could hear her grandmother crying. I felt so sorry for Mrs Quintyne, having to sit there and see her lovely granddaughter in such pain. It made me want to cry as I watched them, but the nurse pulled the curtain across and said, 'She's going to be fine, Lisa.'

Freed from the mask, I suddenly started talking. I told Simon, the ambulance-driving policeman who had stayed at my bedside, that we'd had a teddy bears' picnic and that I had to go to Brownies and aerobics. I said I must find Mum – if I couldn't, who would tell her? And how would Marc know what had happened? I didn't realise then that the news was already being broadcast on TV and radio. I was reassured somehow, while the nurse was wrapping my arm in something and things were being pumped into me from all directions. One after another, doctors came in and introduced themselves, asked my name, then looked at my head and back.

The picture of Ahmed's face flashed into my mind and I asked, 'Where's Ahmed?' I was told he must have gone in another ambulance and I thought, 'That's because he's dead and they've taken the dead ones away in another ambulance.' I lay on the bed thinking I could have done more and it should have been me that had died. How would I bear it if children had died and I lived? I asked the nurse if the children were all right and she said she'd get someone to find out for me.

Simon never left my side and I carried on talking so much that I thought I'd chatter him and the nurse to death. He asked my mum later if I always talked that much. I thought that was funny, because I know for a fact that I hardly ever stop talking. But he and the nurse dealt with me so well – they were both a credit to their professions. The nurse was slowly taking my clothes off and handing them to Simon, who put them in a bag. My necklace and watch went in a separate bag. When she was taking off my camisole I said to her, 'Of all the days not to put on matching underwear!'

I'd been given some shots to ease any pain but there was still a throbbing feeling in my left arm, a dull pain which remains with me to this day. I'm so used to it now that it's just part of me, but what's a pain for the rest of my life compared to no life at all? I have God to thank so much for that.

I really needed the toilet so the nurse helped me into a wheelchair. She had to help me to use the toilet too, because I couldn't use my bandaged arms – they felt as if they'd fallen off. While I was in the toilets I looked at myself in the mirror. It didn't look at all like me. My hair had been cut away, my head was still covered in blood and my back was gaping wide open. Then a strange thing happened; I thought I could hear Mum's voice in my head. I said to the nurse, 'I can hear my mum.' We looked out of the door and there stood Mum at the other end of the corridor. I didn't want her to see me in this state, so the nurse took me back to the cubicle to clean my face up.

Pam Shee had phoned to tell Mum what had happened. It was so good that she wasn't alone; Auntie Pam and Auntie Hazel were in the house with her at the time. Mum hadn't been given any details over the phone; she'd only been told I'd been injured at school. Unfortunately, she'd heard a little bit on the radio news on the way to hospital, and thought a machete was a gun and I'd been shot. Mum and Pam were in complete shock and looked as white as sheets as they walked in. I said to them, 'Oh, I'm going to be fine', and then I started to laugh. Simon said to them, 'Isn't she a happy soul?' Mum and Pam couldn't believe my reaction, but I thought it would make it worse for everyone if I lay there crying.

From then on things are more blurred in my memory, maybe because so much was going on or perhaps because the drugs I'd been given were affecting me. I heard that I had to go for an X-ray on my skull and started to worry that I might have brain damage. The nurse never left my side, even standing outside the door of the X-ray room until I came out, then Mum held my hand while I was wheeled to a ward. The nurses there were so warm and friendly, and chatted to me as they took me through the ward into a room of my own. It felt really late at night but it was probably only around five o'clock. I was told they couldn't operate until nine o'clock because I'd eaten so recently, at the picnic. Then different people were coming and going, as well as the nurses. Auntie Jen and her friends arrived, and some of the staff from St Luke's. Dorothy Hawes, in particular, looked in terrible shock, and I tried to tell them I was going to be fine.

One thing that stands out among this blur is my dad's face as he came in; he looked so ill. He'd been mowing the lawn in Auntie Pam's garden, and Mum had phoned Pam's next-door neighbour to ask her to tell him to get to the hospital quickly. By the time he got there the press were outside, so he had great difficulty getting in, then difficulty in finding which ward I was in. He kissed me. Then at last I was able to tell Mum, Dad and Pam what had happened. Mum told me that Clare's mum, Auntie Hazel, was at our house answering the phone; we found out later there were so many calls that as soon as she put the phone down it rang again.

Just when I was beginning to wonder where Marc was, he came in, looking dreadful. He kissed me and sat down right next to me. He didn't move or talk for a long time, but just kept staring at me. I felt so sorry for him. I looked up and saw Nici and Clare staring at me in shock. I was beginning to realise that this was worse for the people close to me than it was for me. I wondered why everyone else looked so ill, not realising at the time how ill I looked. Marc had been watching tennis at home, and hadn't heard the news of the attack, which was on the other channel. He didn't know anything about it until Nici and Clare knocked on his door and told him what had happened. Apparently he dropped his yoghurt and ran outside to Nici's car. I couldn't imagine how he must have felt; I was just so happy he was next to me.

Everyone who arrived told me how crazy it was outside, with the press rushing up to ask them if they knew any of the victims. I thought, 'I'm not a victim; I'm Lisa Potts.' I was pleased that so many people were coming to see me; I wouldn't have liked it if I'd been left alone to rest. I needed as many people as possible to talk to – and I was certainly doing a lot of that. There was just one person missing and that was my brother, who was in his final months of his PhD at Nottingham. I asked Mum if he'd been told and she just said she was sure he would know by now. Lee arrived before seven o'clock that night with his flatmate who had driven him down from Nottingham. He had heard on the 5.40 television news that the school involved in the attack was St Luke's in Wolverhampton. He'd rung home and spoken to Auntie Hazel, who told him to get to New Cross Hospital as soon as he could. I don't know how fast his flatmate must have driven to get him there so quickly, but I was very pleased to see him.

So many people were crushed into my tiny room, and the nurses were so patient and kind, considering how much they had to deal with. I'd found out some news about the children, but I still kept asking one of the nurses to find out the latest. She came back to tell me they were doing fine. I felt unbelievably happy to know that the three injured children, Ahmed, Francesca and Reena, had not died, and that none of the others had been physically hurt. It was the most amazing feeling which I can't describe. I knew the three would still be in terrible pain and would have awful scars, but to know that they were going to live was wonderful.

Just before nine o'clock I had to go up for surgery, so most people were starting to leave. Before I was wheeled away, the vicar from St Luke's came to visit me, and he read a Bible passage which was extremely comforting. It was from Romans 8, verses 31–39, and it finished with the words: 'I am convinced that neither death nor life, neither angels nor demons, neither the present nor the future, nor any powers, neither height nor depth, nor anything else in all creation, will be able to separate us from the love of God that is in Christ Jesus our Lord.'

The nurse said it was time for me to go and I gave everyone a kiss and hug. They all looked so worried but I was feeling fine. I was about to go in the lift when I saw my friend Emma coming out of the other lift. I asked the nurses if they could stop so I could reassure Emma that I was going to be all right. As we arrived outside the operating theatre we had to wait because Francesca was just being wheeled out. I felt so upset as she passed me; her eyes were shut, but I couldn't see the rest of her face because she had some mesh across it.

Then it was my turn to go into theatre. The mask was put over my face and I said, 'I will shut up now.' I heard the echoes, 'Shut up, shut up, shut up . . .' and then it all went black.

PART THREE

AFTER

6 The Search for the Attacker

I regained consciousness at just after one in the morning, having undergone four hours of surgery. On my left hand I had four severed tendons, one of which was severed twice, and there was a severed tendon in my right index finger. I had a plate put in my left arm in which I had a severely fractured ulna bone. My skull had been chipped and on my back there were two lacerations, one by the left shoulder and the other down the centre of my back, very close to my spine.

When I came round, my hands felt like weights, and I realised that both were in heavy splints with bandages around them. I was taken up to the ward and, still waiting for me there, were Mum, Dad, Lee, Pam and Marc. I tried to make them laugh, lifting up my arms and saying, 'Hello boys.' It didn't work. They all still looked shocked and ill. I felt very sleepy, and can only remember them kissing me and saying they'd see me later in the morning, before I fell asleep.

Next time I woke I thought I was at home, and couldn't understand why I felt so weak and couldn't move my arms at all. I opened my eyes and discovered I was in hospital with my arms hanging in two stirrups above my head. I was dazed and not really sure why I was there. Then a nurse came in and said, 'Good morning, Lisa,' and I suddenly remembered all that had happened. I felt frightened because of it, yet numb at the same time. Immediately, I asked 'How are the children? Is Ahmed OK?' And the nurse said she'd heard they were doing well. I needed the toilet desperately. Two nurses somehow had to lift me onto a bedpan without me having to sit up. They were so funny and cheerful while they attempted the impossible; they treated me as if nothing had happened to me, which I appreciated. We were all laughing as I asked them, 'How on earth am I going to do a wee in that?' In the end they had to take my arms out of the stirrups and angle me against a pile of pillows. Twenty minutes later I still couldn't perform, even though they tried turning on taps and singing songs about water. They told me that shock could have that effect. Sitting there, I was suddenly hit by the enormity of what had happened the day before. I realised I could have died, and said to the nurses, 'I can't believe I'm sitting on this bedpan and that I've survived such a terrible attack.' Yet I still felt as if it had only happened to the children, not to me.

Eventually I managed to use the bedpan, and when the nurses had tidied me up, the hospital's Medical Director came to talk to me. He said there were a lot of press outside who had waited all night, and they needed a statement from me. If I could answer his few questions, he would relay my words to them, then they would leave me alone. I told him briefly about the attack, and said I was in pain but otherwise felt fine. As soon as he'd gone to report back to the press, I had a visitor from the church where I'd helped with the young people the previous weekend. It was strange to think it was less than two days since I'd been with them. At the youth group the previous evening, they'd made me a card. I was really touched that he'd come to see me. Little did I know that the card he brought would be the first of six thousand.

Before I knew any more, Mum, Dad, Lee and Pam were in the room, although I don't remember them coming in. Lee fed me my breakfast, as he was to do every day while I was in hospital. That day I had over forty visitors, and I told my story over and over again. Flowers, fruit baskets, cards, letters and even teddy bears started to arrive by the sackful – many from people I didn't know. I couldn't believe what was happening. I asked Dad to put on the TV, and there was my face staring back at me. It was a peculiar feeling. The picture they kept showing was one that had appeared in the Wolverhampton *Express & Star* a month before, when I'd done a four-hour aerobics session to raise money for Cystic Fibrosis. I asked Mum how they'd got my picture, and she told me the press had been waiting at the house for them when they returned from hospital in the early hours of the morning. Before that, they'd been knocking on doors in our road to find out different things about me. They were still outside the hospital and had stopped Dad on the way in to ask if he was coming to see me, and to ask if he could arrange an interview for them. I said, 'Why me?' Dad said, 'Lisa, you're a heroine – a national one.'

Yesterday I was described as 'a victim'; today I was 'a heroine'. This was the first time I'd heard myself called a heroine, and I thought it was funny. I said to Dad, 'Don't be so soft, I'm not a heroine. I've just been attacked, that's all. It will all die down once they've spoken to me.' I realised I must be of interest to the press, but I really believed that it would only last a few days. I still believed it, even when Dad showed me all the papers with my photo on the front page. One of the headlines read 'Saved by the arms of an angel.' I laughed my head off at that one – me, an angel! Try telling Mum and Dad that when I'm in a bad mood!

The scene on the TV changed to the nursery. There was the playground, with the teddy bears lying on the ground. The one at the front of the picture was my teddy. I found it so difficult to believe that this had happened in the nursery where I worked. Then a picture of a man appeared, and the reporter said this was the man police were searching for. They had been looking for him in the block of flats where he lived, Villiers House, which overlooks the school. Mum asked me if that was the man who attacked me, but I didn't recognise him at first. The man who attacked me was wearing a trilby hat, and I couldn't yet imagine him without one. Dad showed me his photograph in the papers, under the headline 'Machete man still on the run'. I stared at the photo, trying to picture him with a hat on, and suddenly I knew it was him. As I read on, I became frightened. This man hadn't been found and he might be coming to the hospital to find me.

Later on a clinical psychologist came to speak to me, and we went through what had happened. Then CID officers arrived to write a statement with me. The psychologist stayed in as well, in case I had any problems when I had to go through the whole attack in detail. But it was all right, and it felt good to talk about it so slowly from start to finish. I told them as much as I could remember, but it wasn't for weeks afterwards that I started to remember more detail. The psychologist told me it was normal not to remember everything, as I was in shock. When I had to sign my name at the end of the statement I had to hold the pen in my mouth as both arms were hanging in stirrups.

Still more visitors arrived, from Brownies, church, school and dancing school. The staff started to limit them to a maximum of ten minutes because there was such a queue waiting to come in. The nurses were so tolerant, never complaining about the constant stream of people, but just coming in occasionally to see if everything was all right. They made sure I got some rest if I needed it, but I think they knew that I needed people around me. They also kept me informed every couple of hours about how the children were getting on, which put my mind at rest. Even though I was in pain and I couldn't move my arms or do anything, at least those three children were alive. That was the main thing.

After my brother had given me my tea, Nicola arrived to tell me what was happening at St Luke's. She said all the staff had to leave the school after the attack with police escorts, and my car had been driven home by the police. They had all been given a few days off, and the school wouldn't reopen until the following Monday. The nursery, though, wouldn't be opening until after the summer holidays. It would take some time to clean up all the blood and resurface the play area, and already there was talk of new security fences being put up. Photographers, cameramen and reporters were still packing the road outside the school, and the police had had to close the road off.

The situation with the media was getting out of hand at the hospital too. Later that afternoon the hospital's press officer, Jock Gallagher, came to talk to me about giving an interview, as they all wanted to speak to me. I asked how many people from the media were out there; he told me there were too many to count, and that a special room had been set up for them. Security staff had been placed on my ward because one of the reporters had tried to pose as a doctor to get in, and another had said he was my uncle. It wasn't considered safe to have my name up on the board at the front of the ward to say which room I was in. The staff decided to give the impression that my room was empty, and had put the words 'Broken Bed' against my room number.

Not all of the press would come to my room, Jock Gallagher said. There would be just one TV cameraman and reporter, who would pass everything on to the other stations, as well as one photographer and reporter from my local paper, the *Express & Star*. He said if I was up to it, I should do it, then the media would leave me alone. I remembered hearing that somewhere before, not so many hours earlier. I felt as if I wanted to help, but what I couldn't tell him was that I was still worried about the attacker who was on the loose and might come looking for me. I couldn't seem to get that thought out of my head, so I told Jock I'd have to think about the press coming in. I talked to my family and Marc about it, and eventually decided I would go ahead. It might even help in the search for the man.

When Jock came in later for my decision I told him I'd decided it would be easier for everyone if I co-operated. The nurses came in to prepare me, brushing my hair and putting me into a dressing-gown. They were keeping my spirits high, making me laugh and telling me to mention their names on TV. When the media appeared, Mum, Dad, Lee and Pam had gone for something to eat, having not eaten all day. Marc chose to wait outside, keeping well out of the way. The four people standing in my room were strangers; I didn't realise I'd get to know them well and would see much more of them over the next year. They didn't outstay their welcome on their first visit, but accepted my brief answers to their questions about the attack, then wished me well, and left. It wasn't as bad as I'd feared.

Marc and I switched on the news later and heard that

the man, Horrett Campbell, had been found in a dry-riser cupboard in the Villiers House flats, twenty-eight hours after the attack. The police had been about to call off their search when one of the dog-handlers had found him and had quickly shouted out to his colleagues. There was a film of the police running in with shields and helmets, then leading out a man covered with a blue blanket. He looked so small underneath that blanket, compared to all the police swarming around him. The machete hadn't been found, but he had some screwdrivers and a smaller knife on him when the police discovered him. There was a crowd of people in the background shouting and jeering. I felt so relieved he had been found, but I simply couldn't accept any of it was happening. Surely this nightmare would end any minute.

After that I appeared on the screen, as they showed part of the interview I'd given so recently. I watched myself, but I couldn't believe that the person on the screen really was me. It didn't even look like me; it was someone who was extremely pale and drawn in the face, with dark circles under the eyes and greasy, unwashed hair. That was not me – but then if it wasn't, who else could it be? It was all so unreal. Next we saw Ahmed, from hospital in Birmingham, where he had been taken because of the severity of his head injury. The poor little boy was just lying there, his head half shaven on top and stitches running across the top of his head. I wanted to cry, but I held the tears back. Less than thirty hours before, he had been running around with his sister, enjoying his very first taste of nursery. His dad, sitting next to him, spoke to the camera: 'Miss Potts was badly injured but she saved their lives.' Me, Lisa Potts, saving lives? Perhaps I did. But to this day, and forever, I know what I did was instinctive. I just thank God that he gave me the instinct to run back for those children. I was no heroine – just a human being fighting for the lives of other human beings, for the lives of those more innocent and helpless than me. Could I have kept still and watched those children die in front of me? Would that have been easier than to try and save them?

The picture changed to Reena, lying in her hospital bed with a cut across her face; then a photograph of Francesca, the cut across her face even bigger than Reena's. How could that man do such a thing to these children? I wanted to reach out and hug them. I felt so guilty after I had watched the TV that night, and after everyone had gone home I couldn't rid myself of that feeling of guilt. If only my hand had been that little bit higher or closer, none of them would have been injured. I felt so ill with the feeling of guilt that I had to call the nurse, because I realised I was literally going to be sick. That feeling remains with me to this day, as much as people keep telling me I did all I could. Even when the children's parents kept telling me I saved lives and did all I could, I didn't believe them. The feeling isn't as bad now, since I started to have counselling some months later, and I hope one day it will finally leave me.

7 Facing the Media

When my family arrived early the next morning, Lee said, 'Wait till you see all the mail you've got!' In came a huge sackful, just for me. That was the start of things to come. People wrote such wonderful things, and children from schools across the country sent me pictures. I had letters from people who had been stabbed, which gave me so much comfort. I was overwhelmed by such a wonderful response, and so grateful to all the people who contacted me. In the previous couple of days I had started to lose my faith in humanity, but through this support I was being shown, I realised that for every bad person there are thousands of kind, caring people.

So many flowers were pouring in that soon Mum had to start putting some in the ward outside, and she took some to church the following Sunday, because people couldn't get into my room for flowers. They were arriving from all over the country, as well as from the media, local companies, the Mayor, and my own friends, family and neighbours. People have asked if I went off flowers after that, because they would always be a reminder. Yes, they are a reminder, but the beautiful colours brightened up my life so much in hospital. They will always remind me not only of the bad thing that happened, but of the many kind people who cared about me. They also remind me to value my life, because I might never have seen a flower again. I never take flowers for granted now.

Mr Fraser, my doctor, brought the occupational therapist and physiotherapist with him that morning when he came to see me. They were going to see if I could start to move my shoulders and legs a little in bed, because they didn't want me to stiffen up. I wasn't strong enough to get up, but I really wanted to, especially when other patients in the ward came to visit me. I knew that if the doctor gave his permission, I could go later to see Francesca and Reena in the children's ward. He said I could, and I was so excited as the nurses put me into a wheelchair. I couldn't wait to see them both. On the way down everyone we met was chatting to me and telling me how brave I was; it took us a long time to get down to the ward. The nurse who was taking me was so patient, but I felt awful that she had to keep stopping for me, yet there was no way I could just ignore everyone. It felt strange to realise that although I didn't know any of these people, they all knew who I was.

When we eventually arrived in the children's ward and the nurse pushed me into the playroom, I couldn't believe my eyes. There was Reena, playing happily with her brother. She was still hooked up to a drip, like me, but she seemed so cheerful. As soon as her mum saw me she ran over and kissed me; she kept saying, 'Thank you so much, Miss Potts.' I asked her how she was feeling, as she too had been hit on the head. Then Reena turned round to see what was going on. She stared at me with her huge, frightened eyes – then she started screaming. I couldn't believe it. What had I done? She wouldn't stop, so her mum had to take her out of the room.

I'd been so excited about coming to visit Reena, and it upset me terribly that she had reacted to me in this way.

The clinical psychologist told me later that Reena would relate some of the attack to me because I was the adult there when it happened. 'Yes,' I thought, 'I was the adult, so I should have been protecting the children. They should not have been injured; if only it had been just me.' I kept thinking I should have done more than I did. Yet at the same time I knew that I *couldn't* have done any more. The 'if only, if only' feeling wouldn't go away; it haunted me for another year. Since then I've struggled to come to terms with it, but I know I'll probably have to live with it for the rest of my life.

I wondered how Francesca would react. She was in her hospital room with her mum, dad and grandma. They welcomed me, but Francesca seemed reluctant. She didn't cry, but neither did she talk to me; she just stared at me. Her wound was much bigger than Reena's, and she'd had to have a plate inserted into her jaw, but she wasn't complaining about the pain. When I got back to my own room I wanted to break down and cry, but I couldn't because there were at least thirty people waiting to see me. They were waiting patiently in a queue, and I felt so grateful that all these people were willing to stand there just for me. Once the nurse had helped me from the wheelchair onto the bed, checked my blood pressure and given me painkillers, I was ready for the first group of visitors to come in. For the rest of the day I went over and over the story, which helped release some of the tension I was feeling.

The days in hospital seem now to be rolled into one. Sacks of letters, cards and presents kept arriving, and whoever was in the room with me opened them for me. Visitors kept on queuing to see me; it seemed as if everyone I'd ever known came to the hospital, plus some I didn't know. Even the Mayor of Wolverhampton and the Bishops of Wolverhampton and Lichfield appeared at my bedside. I had visits from the police every day, and the clinical psychologist, and after a few days the physiotherapist helped me to start walking a little way. It tired me out, and I was still in a lot of pain, but all I wanted to do was get out of bed and prance around as I normally did. Each day until they were discharged I visited Francesca and Reena, and at the weekend they came to visit me, to say goodbye. Francesca smiled, but Reena started to cry. I felt so sad, but knew that when I got back to school I could start to work with her slowly. My parents, Lee, Marc, Pam, Clare, Nici and Dawn stayed quite late every evening, always leaving in time for me to have half an hour alone with Marc. This was the only time I got to speak to them at all. I don't know how the nurses and doctors found the time to care for me, but they did.

Each day the newspapers made horrific reading for the whole country. On the first day, the headline above the picture of Ahmed lying in hospital with his teddy bear read 'How do we explain this?' I thought that it would never be explained, but that I wasn't going to lose my faith. It's man, not God, that does these evil things. Two days later the story below the headline 'Copycat maniac' shocked the country again. I just couldn't believe that Horrett Campbell had cuttings of the Dunblane massacre and the Tasmanian gunman in his flat. I couldn't get Dunblane out of my mind that day, knowing that those children and a teacher didn't survive, and realising that if Campbell had had a gun, we would probably have been dead, too. I felt for those people at Dunblane so much; the attack at St Luke's, happening only four months after their tragedy, must have stirred up some terrible emotions for them. When Denise came to see me later, it cheered me up to be told that among the cards St Luke's had received from schools all over the country, there was one from Dunblane Primary.

Three days after the attack I read in the *Express & Star* that thirty-two-year-old Horrett Campbell had appeared in court accused of the attempted murder of three children and four adults. He was handcuffed to two police officers during a six-minute hearing. The report said he was charged with trying to kill Lisa Potts, parents Wendy Willington, Azra Rafiq and Reena's mother Surinder Kaur Chopra, all aged twenty-nine, Reena Chopra and Francesca Quintyne-Peart, both aged four, and Ahmed Pervez, aged three. I kept reading it over and over again. 'To kill Lisa Potts,' it said. He was trying to kill me. It was frightening to know he could easily have achieved his intention.

A television interview with Taishion made me realise that it wasn't just the three injured children who would be affected for the rest of their lives by the attack. Taishion said, 'A man hit Miss Potts with a machete,' and I wondered how much he and the others had seen. Some may just have seen a man jump the fence before they were taken to safety. Others would have witnessed it all – and the group that huddled under me as Campbell stood above us, hitting me with the knife, must have been affected more than many of the others. I know children are resilient, but no-one can know what effect the experience will have on them in the future.

I loved it when some of the children and their parents came to see me. The children were quite shocked when they first came in. They must have thought it was weird to see their nursery nurse in bed with her arms up in slings. But as soon as I started talking to them, their silent wide-eyed stares changed to comfortable chatter. I asked their parents to lift them onto the bed. I really wanted to give them big hugs, but I couldn't, so I had to make do with kissing them on the cheek. I wanted them to know they were going to be all right, and so was I.

When Marium came to see me, though, she wasn't a bit upset. She surprised me by jumping up on my bed straight away and starting to chat about Ahmed's injury and all the presents he'd been sent. She brought me balloons and a mug with the words 'To a wonderful teacher'. Her auntie kept on thanking me and telling me I was special. But the words that will remain with me for ever were Marium's: 'You saved my brother and I love you, Miss Potts.' She put her arms round my neck and hugged me, and when she left I wanted to be left alone. I hadn't really cried until then, but to hear those powerful words from a four-year-old was so moving.

Some twins from the nursery brought me a piece of their birthday cake. Their dad told me the press had stopped them outside to ask if they were coming to see me, and they'd been interviewed on television. People from the media were stopping almost everyone, asking them to give me their card and requesting an interview. I was offered ridiculous amounts of money, but I decided there was no way I was going to take money for my story. It wasn't a story about me; it was about an awful tragedy that had happened to the children, staff and parents in a small school. I couldn't make money out of a tragedy in which innocent children nearly lost their lives – and apart from anything else, I wouldn't have appreciated the money because I hadn't earned it. I was not going to cash in on it for myself. If people wanted to give money to the school, that was different. I have kept to that decision to this day, and I'm so glad about it because I feel I know where I stand with the press and they know where they stand with me.

But while I didn't give in to cheque-book journalism, I

was really touched by the money people were sending as gifts. There were cheques for £5 or £10, sometimes for the school, sometimes for me. One little boy sent me 25p, which he said was half his pocket money. I was determined when my hands got better to write and thank all these people.

The media couldn't be put off for ever, and on the Sunday, six days after the attack, Jock Gallagher came to see me again. The press were not leaving the hospital and were now even more keen to speak to me, as St Luke's was opening again the next morning and they wanted to know how I felt about it. I agreed to a few interviews, including GMTV live the next morning, and Sky TV in the afternoon. But after Marc left that night I began to feel sad. I was anxious about the children going back to school, and I really wanted to be there myself. It made me feel a little better to think that the nursery wasn't opening until after the holidays, so I didn't feel I was missing out quite so much. Sadly, though, the nursery should have been going on a trip to Telford Town Park the next day and we'd been looking forward to it. I hardly slept that night, but the night nurses came in to chat to me, trying to make me laugh.

In the morning I was up very early for a bath and hair wash, to make me look more presentable for the interviews. I was like a child, having to have everything done for me by the nurses, but they never once made me feel useless. I had the stitches taken out of my head, then the doctor, Mr Fraser, came to see me. It was still only eight o'clock when Jock Gallagher came in to help set up the interview. I didn't really feel nervous, considering it was my first live interview. It went well, although it felt strange to be looking into a camera and talking to it, not seeing anyone. People watching could see Eamonn Holmes asking the questions and me answering them, but I just saw a camera and heard a voice.

Along with many thousands throughout the country, I watched the children's emotional assembly on television. Denise talked to the children, and prayers were said for the people injured in the attack. I wanted to cry as I watched their little faces praying, and was so upset to see Kath, the nursery nurse, looking so poorly. I felt for all the teachers there, who must have been going through so much themselves, and then would have to deal with the children's emotions throughout the day.

The day went quickly for me. I did a couple of live news broadcasts at lunchtime, then in the afternoon I was taken into the hospital garden for the interviews. It was a very warm day, and the nurse wheeled me out for each interview, then back in again so I wouldn't get too hot. The press and TV crews kept asking Marc to talk, but he was too shy. He said he didn't mind standing next to me, but he wouldn't speak. I didn't mind at all – that's his character, and I didn't want to force him. Later in the afternoon our local BBC presenter Sue Beardsmore interviewed me in one of the day rooms.

I watched television whenever I could, to see coverage of the children at school. Although the day had been busy, I felt so lonely, especially when I saw that some of the nursery children were going in after all. It had been decided that as many of them as wanted to could spend time playing in the school that week, so they wouldn't feel so frightened returning to school after the long summer holidays. Some people expressed the view that it was too soon to reopen the school, but I didn't agree. At least this way the children could get back to some degree of normality instead of having the build-up of many weeks' anxiety before they faced school again.

Mum and Pam started to take the flowers and presents home because I was hopefully going to be discharged in two days. I didn't really feel excited about it, because I still felt weak and couldn't walk far without feeling exhausted. I did more interviews and had lots of visitors on the Tuesday, and by the evening I felt frightened about leaving the next morning. I'd been in a secure environment and going back to the real world seemed like another ordeal. But I knew I was going to have to face each problem as it came up, and to take one step at a time on the road to normality. I had decided I was going to get through this – the attack wasn't going to hold me down and stop my life from being happy, as it used to be.

That night I dreamed I was locked in a small glass room and was forced to watch through the glass as all the children were slashed with a machete. They were all killed, and I was the only survivor. I woke up, sweating and frightened, but relieved that it hadn't really happened. It was my first nightmare, but it was far from being my last. Although in the morning I still felt worried about leaving, I didn't want to show my feelings because I thought they would pass as soon as I was back home. The nurses had already helped me dress by the time Marc arrived to pack up the rest of my things. Mum had brought in a long black flowery dress for me to leave in, obviously wanting me to feel pretty for the first time I was dressed in nine days. Mr Fraser came in to see if I was fit enough to go home. Then I said goodbye to him and all the nurses. We thanked them for looking after me so well, and Mum gave them chocolates and a card. As I left, I thought, 'What a wonderful job these nurses do every day, and so much of it goes unnoticed.'

Marc packed his car full of my presents and flowers, and I went in Pam's car with Mum. The nurses asked if I wanted to go in a wheelchair to the car, but I said no. I thought I could walk, if I went slowly, but it took such a long time, especially when I was still stopping to talk to well-wishers. By the time I'd got to the end of the corridor I was shattered. Again Mum offered me a wheelchair but I said I'd make it to the car, although a large part of me wanted to say yes. I needed to show myself I could do this; I could walk.

When we got to the hospital entrance I was about to give in, but I saw a little girl from nursery walking towards me. I was glad to sit on a bench in the sun and talk to her, even though it was agony to sit down. April's mum gave me some chocolates and said she was sorry not to have visited before; she didn't realise I was leaving hospital so soon. I tried to put April on my lap, but couldn't, so her mum lifted her up on my knee. After she'd finished staring at me, April hugged and chatted to me. By the time they left, I realised that there was no need to feel scared about leaving the hospital, as I had all these children to look forward to seeing when I got back to school. I had no idea, then, how long it would be before I was fit enough to go back.

At home, Pam helped me out of the car, then Mum and Pam had to hold me up as they led me to the front door. Mum opened the door and there was Dad, putting the hoover away, as he had been when I came out of New Cross Hospital sixteen years before. Lee was there, too, and they both welcomed me. I walked into the living room and was hit by such a strange brightness. It was full of flowers and balloons, all of which had been in hospital with me, but at home they looked wrong. It made the house look like a florist's shop and the smell was overpowering. All of a sudden I saw myself back in hospital. I didn't like it, but I didn't say anything to anyone. I thought, 'Oh well, they're making the place look nice, I suppose.' Mum helped me into a chair and put my feet on a pouffe. I said, 'Lee, where're the chocolates?' He found them, unwrapped them and I ate the lot.

Almost straight away the door-knocking began. It wasn't the press – they thought I was still in hospital, so left me in peace for my first week at home. The people who poured into the house now were family, neighbours and friends from school, college, church, dancing and Brownies. At one point that day there were twenty-six people in the house. I loved every minute. I didn't have to move, everyone came to me. They brought presents – chocolates, perfume, more teddy bears. Mum made everyone cups of tea and kept filling plates with biscuits. The phone seemed to go non-stop. At least thirty people rang on my first day home. The whole house was buzzing; it was like one big festival. The support was unbelievable. And that was just the beginning – people didn't stop coming.

Everyone was fussing round me, Mum was busy putting duvets under me, and it felt so nice. But when it came to bedtime and I tried to walk upstairs, my back was really painful. Mum got me ready for bed and then left me alone with Marc for ten minutes. Marc tried to cheer me up, because I was in such pain. I had to lie on my side with both hands hanging off the side of the bed. They felt so heavy and painful with a horrible dull ache. But as soon as I was left alone I went straight to sleep and slept for about ten hours.

From that day Mum had to look after me for weeks, with lots of help from close friends. In the mornings Clare or Dawn came round to help get me up, and Nici came to help later. I couldn't do anything for myself. Friends and family were called on to do everything, including helping me on the toilet. When I bathed I had to have my hands in plastic bags, and Clare sat on the toilet seat and talked to me, then helped me when I struggled to get out.

Mum and Pam took me to hospital on the day after I was discharged for the first of many outpatients appointments. It was my first time out in public, and as soon as I walked in people started to look at me. It felt so strange to hear my own name ringing in my ears and to overhear people saying to Mum, 'That's Lisa, isn't it?' I had no idea that this would carry on wherever I went. I thought these people only recognised me because it was at the local hospital and the attack was so recent. Pat Jones, the Director of Nursing, told us to go straight through so that my name wouldn't have to be called out.

The doctor took the splints off my arms and said I was doing very well, then sent me for an X-ray on my arm. The police photographer was there to take a picture of my arm, hand, head and back. Having someone taking photographs of my body felt like I'd died and they had to have pictures for a pathologist's report. They were in fact to be used in evidence. The Sister came in to pull the stitches out of my back and arm. It wasn't painful, but it was a horrible feeling as the twenty-five stitches were pulled out of my back one by one. I insisted on looking at my arm and hand. It was the first time I'd seen my arm since I'd looked at it cut open. It was an awful sight, so thin and wasted, with its black lines of thread. The Sister said, 'You see, it's not that bad, is it?' I didn't feel sad or unhappy; my only thought was that they'd done a really amazing job. She started to pull the stitches out one at a time; there were about forty in my left hand and arm, and fifteen in my right hand. I tried to make a joke of it. I could hear Mum talking to Pam outside the curtain. She kept calling to me, 'Are you sure you don't want me with you?' and I replied, 'Mum, I'm not a baby,' even though I knew she was so worried about me.

I had to go to the plastering room next and I assured them I was all right to walk. But I had to wait, so I was put onto a bed, where I immediately fell asleep. When I eventually got there the staff said I could have whatever colour cast I wanted, so I chose a luminous one – the children would enjoy seeing it when I visited them. I couldn't stop thinking about the children. They were constantly in my mind, whether I was at the hospital or talking to visitors at home. I was updated about their progress daily, but I still wanted to know more about how they were. As it turned out I didn't see them for eight weeks; they needed time to recover too.

Then it was time to meet Steve and Esther, the occupational therapists. Because the tendons had been severed I had to learn to use my fingers again, so the plaster cast went down to my knuckles, leaving my fingers free. At occupational therapy I had traction put on the top of the cast on my left arm. I was fascinated by the contraption. There were silver wheels on a metal plate attached to the back of my fingers by elastic bands which ran halfway up my forearm. I had to learn to pull my fingers down and the elastic bands would pull them back up again. On my first attempts I couldn't move them at all, but I knew it would be all right in time. I was given an appointment for the next day and went home exhausted.

Marc had been given two weeks' compassionate leave from work, and the next day he took me for my occupational therapy appointment. He and Pam began to take it in turns to drive me to hospital, which was no mean feat as I had appointments every other day and the hospital was seven miles away. They never complained. And I was always treated like a VIP at hospital too. I never stopped feeling guilty at my special treatment. Other people should have been seen before me, but I was always called in first. That day was the end of term at St Luke's. I still thought I'd be going back to work after the summer holidays, so I felt as if I was breaking up for six weeks' holiday too. I had no idea then that I wouldn't be fit to work by September.

Lee had to go back to Nottingham and we were both upset that he was leaving. He had been feeding me more than anyone else, but now my plaster cast was on I had three free fingers which worked on my right hand, and I was starting to learn to do some things for myself. I could feed myself with a spoon if Mum mashed the food up first, and with a great effort I learned to unbutton my clothes, brush my teeth and even put on some make-up. It was the start of my new independence.

At the weekend I asked Marc if we could go out into the garden. Dawn was there with Ashley, and Clare and Nicola too. It was a hot day, and I sat there with a cap on to protect me from the sun, while being pampered by everyone. Marc read a book to me while Dawn shaved my legs because I was complaining about how hairy they were. Then Dawn and Clare picked the dried blood out of my fingernails and cleaned them with cotton wool and lotion. Mum usually wiped my hands with a flannel, but my nails were still dirty – as my fingers were so delicate and painful, they were difficult to clean properly. Suddenly there was a loud bang. I've no idea what it was, but it terrified me and I asked if we could go back inside.

Along with the masses of visitors who still poured in was someone from Victim Support. I filled in a form and she said I'd get an award from Criminal Injuries Compensation. I also had a visit from the clinical psychologist, who was to visit every week to start with, although at the time I didn't feel I needed that sort of help. I'd have hated it if no-one had been to visit. If Mum had told people to leave me alone I'd have asked her what she was talking about. At one point Auntie Jen said to Mum, 'Let her have a bit of peace.' But Mum said, 'Ask her – she doesn't want it.' And she was right, I didn't want peace and quiet. The place would have felt like a morgue without all the visitors and I liked them being there. But the huge difficulty about it was that people like Marc, Clare and Dawn began to be pushed further away. I talked to all my visitors, but wasn't expected to talk to close friends in the same way. These were the people who were doing everything for me, yet I was aware of them having to take a back seat. I felt powerless to do anything about it.

The media left me alone until Monday evening, five days after I came out of hospital. It had in one sense been a quiet five days, although I was constantly busy with visitors, but it wasn't until the press started coming that I realised how idyllic my first days at home had been. That Monday the hairdresser came round, and my friend Louise gave me a pedicure and waxed my eyebrows. There were lots of people at the door as usual, and in the evening when Dad answered the knock it was a journalist from *The Sun*. Dad let him in and Mum treated him like any other visitor, giving him a cup of tea and a piece of cake. He was the first of many people from the media who received Mum's hospitality. On one occasion she made bacon sandwiches for a whole group of journalists. Months later a journalist on his fourth visit said that he loved coming to our house because we made him feel so welcome, whereas he was usually turned away when he knocked on people's doors.

The first of countless hundreds of interviews took place that night. I talked about what had happened and told him how I felt. It didn't bother me to talk about it. It was a story and people wanted to know. I hadn't done anything wrong, so why not? I wouldn't say I enjoyed it, but I didn't hate it either. This first interview was the time I started to talk about how I felt about what had happened. I found it helpful to express my feelings to people I didn't know. It was easier to talk to the press than to Marc or my parents, because they knew me so well.

Dad bought a copy of *The Sun* with the double-page spread all about me. Louise had balanced a teddy, one of the gifts I'd been sent, on my shoulder for the photograph, and there I was, smiling out at everyone. But I didn't feel as if it *was* me. It was about a Lisa Potts who was somebody else, not the normal Lisa Potts. But then I wasn't ever going to see the other Lisa Potts again.

That interview was nothing compared to the next day, when Mum got me up and dressed me in my Guiding uniform. Apparently the Guiding Association had phoned on Monday to say they were coming to see me with a surprise. That Tuesday morning two Guiding Commissioners arrived with a framed Certificate of Merit for Exceptional Bravery. Suddenly the media started arriving. A photographer from the Wolverhampton *Express & Star* was followed by many others, including photographers from the *Evening Mail*, the *Daily Mail* and *The Sun*, and even the local TV stations. I don't know how they found out – I suppose they were told this was going to be happening. The Commissioners presented me with the award in the garden, in front of flashing lights, cameras and a sea of faces. I did interviews for radio, TV and newspapers, telling them all how exciting it was to be given a lovely certificate. I don't remember what I told them, but reading the papers the next day, I'd said: 'I can't believe this award. I don't know why they are giving it to me. I am going to put it in a frame and it will take pride of place in the living room.' I had no idea at all that this was to be only the first of many awards. I thought it was a one-off – I'd been given a certificate, I'd had some photos taken, and that was an end to it. Before they left, one journalist asked for my phone number so he could check he had his story right. I gave it to him, which was the biggest mistake. They all got hold of it and from then on I wasn't left alone.

One of the people there was Peter Wilson from BBC *Midlands Today*. He said he'd like to do a piece on me, and asked if he could ring on Thursday to discuss his plans. When he rang, he said he'd be interested in making some short films on what had happened to me, to be broadcast at the beginning of September. I thought, as usual, 'Why not?' I was on six weeks' holiday from school and I didn't really think of saying I wouldn't do it. Besides, it could help with the healing process if I expressed myself on TV. I agreed to go to Birmingham the following Monday, and to film for most of that week. It seems odd, looking back, that I agreed to do that so soon after the attack, with my hands still in plaster and having regular hospital treatment. Over the next year, Peter Wilson and the cameraman Larry Warr were to become good friends of mine, and I knew I could trust them both. They had a fantastic way of making me laugh when I was feeling down.

Before the filming I had another ordeal to face. Denise had invited me to go to St Luke's that Wednesday with the other staff, just for us to spend an hour together. The police thought it would be better if I was accompanied, so two CID officers, Clive and Jean, drove me to the school. I felt frightened that once I got there I'd relive the whole experience, but I didn't. The police walked me in and all the teachers were waiting in the staff-room. Dorothy Hawes was the only one not there. She'd been to visit me a couple of days before, and I'd been glad to speak with her. She didn't stay with me long; she didn't look well, and was on her way to stay with her brother. The police sat next to me in the staff-room, and we were all very quiet. The atmosphere was sad and miserable. It seemed as if all the staff were still in shock. It certainly wasn't the happy, buzzing school it had been. I felt sad that I'd been given all the publicity while the rest of the staff had been almost forgotten – Dorothy, Nicola, Denise, Kath who'd seen my arm, and Pam Shee who'd had to get the children in and out. I asked about the children, and was told that they came to the school whenever they wanted.

I asked the police if I could go into the nursery. I wanted to go by myself, but Jean said she'd come with me. Linda, the Reception teacher, came too. When we met that day Linda had hugged me, and from then on we formed a good bond. I'd expected the blood to be cleaned up, but otherwise I thought the nursery would look just like it was, with the furniture in the same place and the bright pictures on the walls. But Dorothy had been in, taken everything down and rearranged the furniture. I felt upset because I'd needed to see it as it was. I don't blame Dorothy – it was her way of dealing with it. I suppose she'd wanted to throw things away to get it all out of her mind and start afresh, but it was a shock because it wasn't the way I remembered it.

I wanted to go out into the nursery playground, but when I opened the door I saw all the lovely new play surface had been lifted because of the blood on it. It was as I stepped out onto the cold concrete of the playground that I cried properly for the first time since the attack. Jean told me to let it out, and I tried to explain to her and to Linda how I felt, and told them what I remembered about what had happened, where I'd been trapped, where I'd run. This wasn't the nursery I'd loved, it was a dead place where I'd been attacked and the children had been attacked.

I went away with mixed feelings, wishing I'd not gone, but knowing it was best for me that I *had* gone. I had another good cry all by myself when I got home, and that night I cried again with Marc, who was really supportive. I had to accept that the nursery had changed, but that sad day at school was a setback. I may be wrong, but I feel that if I'd gone back and seen the nursery as it was, I wouldn't have suffered the severe flashbacks I was to have later. The day played on my mind for a couple of weeks afterwards, but I still thought, 'In September it will be back to normal, I'll go back and be that nursery nurse again.'

I'd felt quite happy until I'd gone back to St Luke's – battered about, but not sorry for myself. I suppose I hadn't had time to think about it much. But now a new set of emotions hit me. That weekend when Marc took me to a friend's house for a meal I felt so weak and lost. I was closed in on myself and alone. Other people hadn't been through what I had, so they couldn't be in my world. These feelings weren't there all the time, and I soon began to enjoy myself that night, even though I couldn't eat by myself because of the splints.

The following Monday I went to meet Peter Wilson at the BBC in Birmingham. I wasn't worried about going by myself on the fifty-minute taxi ride. That is, until the taxi turned up, and the driver was wearing a trilby hat, like Horrett Campbell. At first I said I couldn't go, then I calmed down and got in the taxi. I decided to face it head on; if I didn't get in that taxi, what else might I be unable to do in the future? That was the first time the sight of a trilby hat had affected me, but it wouldn't be the last. For the whole of that week I was filming. We did films of me talking about the attack, of Mum washing my face and of Louise giving me a massage. They came to hospital and filmed me there, and I was filmed tap-dancing in the kitchen. It was interesting to see how the camera worked and how Larry, the cameraman, went about the filming. I enjoyed it and it stopped me thinking about the attack and the visit to the nursery.

One of my visitors in the middle of that week was Mike, the youth leader from church. I was due to go to camp ten days later, on 10 August, to help with forty deprived children. Mike said he realised I couldn't go and I wasn't to feel guilty. I asked him what he meant – of course I was going. Why should I stop doing all the things I'd planned because of one man who'd attacked me? On my next visit to occupational therapy I told Steve I was going on the camp and wouldn't be able to come to hospital for a full week. He said I couldn't go, but then said he was joking and of course I could go. But he said I was silly to go away with forty children and warned me not to do anything strenuous.

As soon as I got home I had a phone call from Jock Gallagher, the press officer at New Cross Hospital. He said he had a surprise for me: someone had given me a one-week, all-expenses-paid trip to Disneyland in America. All I could say was, 'What for?' I wondered why I was getting a free holiday. He said he couldn't tell me who had given me the trip, but it was for two people and we were booked to fly out at 6 a.m. on 18 August. I said I wouldn't be able to go because I wasn't getting back from camp until 17 August. I just couldn't miss camp. Then I thought, 'Why not do both?' I told Jock I'd go, and suddenly felt very excited. My parents' reaction didn't match mine, though. Mum said, 'You're joking!' and Dad said, 'No way.' They both pointed out that I had just been through a huge emotional incident, I'd had major surgery, and I was now planning to go away for two weeks, two trips involving forty children and two eight-hour flights. I wondered why they were making such a fuss. I was just being my normal self, I thought.

When they'd calmed down a bit I asked Mum if I could take Marc with me. I phoned him and all he could say, over and over again, was, 'No! Really?' Then he said I'd be worn out, and I said, 'Don't you go on too.' Minutes later the phone rang again, and then again, and the *Express & Star*, as well as the national papers, were asking, 'What's all this about Disneyland?' I wondered how on earth they knew about it, but realised Jock Gallagher must have contacted the press. A couple of hours later the *Express & Star* and *The Sun* took me to be photographed outside St Luke's, and I made the news yet again. That night I sat back and wondered if this was real. Could all this really be happening to me?

I had to face occupational therapy again two days later, this time to tell them I'd be away for two weeks rather than one. Steve had to bring in the doctor to ask if I could have the plaster off a week early. It was arranged that I could have my plaster off before I went to America, but that I should keep the support bandage on and not do anything with my hand while I was away. Now I was in another dilemma: I couldn't go to hospital the week before Disneyland because I was at camp. I rang Mike, who suggested I only went to camp for the first half of the week, then someone would take me home in time for the hospital appointment, and I could stay at home after that. I wasn't having that either. I said I'd be grateful if someone could bring me back for the hospital appointment, but then I was going straight back to camp for the rest of the week.

The week before camp was full of filming, occupational therapy, talking to visitors and opening lots of post, as usual. My faithful 'big sister' and 'little sister', Dawn and

Clare, came to see me every day, as did Marc and Nici, and Lee phoned daily. The media attention had tailed off for a while, except for the local press. I was still in a lot of pain, but I wouldn't let my hands get me down, even though they drove me mad sometimes when they wouldn't do what I wanted them to. The psychologist came round again and asked me questions. I told her I felt frightened but I wasn't going to let it affect my life. It was only a month since the attack, but I wasn't feeling very much. Looking back now, I can see I was still in shock. Mum told me afterwards that I'd often sit and stare, going into my own world even when visitors were with me. I wasn't aware of doing that until 8 August, exactly one month after the attack. I sat down that day for a long time and wondered how this awful thing could have happened to all those sweet little children. I never remember wondering why it had happened to me – whenever I thought about it, it was always in connection with the children. Every night my last thought was for the children; and I'd wake up thinking about them. I never thought about Horrett Campbell at that stage, but then I didn't need to.

The night before camp, 9 August, Clare came to help me pack. She shaved my legs again, and we had a good laugh together. The next morning Christine, one of the youth leaders from church, picked me up and took me to Oswestry to the converted farmhouse I'd visited the previous summer. I couldn't look after myself and the children properly so I shared a room with Christine and just two of the children. We had a fantastic time and I could play all the games and take part in everything except swimming and canoeing.

Halfway through the week Spencer, one of the leaders, took me back to New Cross Hospital where Mr Fraser was going to decide whether the plaster could come off my arm. The *Express & Star* and BBC Midlands were waiting at the hospital to photograph me going in with the plaster on. In the hospital everyone looked at me again – 'That's Lisa Potts' – but as usual I was called straight in, while Spencer stood outside the door like a bodyguard. I looked at my arm as the plaster came off and it looked even thinner than the first time. I couldn't move it at all and I kept staring at it, wondering what had happened. I was sent to occupational therapy, along with Larry and Peter from BBC Midlands. Larry filmed as Esther rubbed cream into my arm to loosen the scar tissue and advised me to keep it in a strap and not to move it – as if I could anyway! The plaster had been taken off about seven days before it should have been; my arm looked so red and the pain was terrible.

At one point I was in so much pain that I said to Larry, 'I'm going to be sick.' He joked, 'Shall I film you being sick, Lisa?' I was, and he didn't. I was looking forward to getting back to camp and felt quite happy, apart from a brief moment of worry about the damage to my forefinger – my writing finger – but I forgot about it after a minute. Before I left, Peter gave me the camera to take to America with me. Marc was going to keep on filming, so there would be a full record of my first few weeks. I don't think Marc was very happy about this, but he agreed to do it. Peter also gave me £100 spending money, courtesy of BBC Midlands. This was one of the few payments I was given by the media, and I certainly didn't ask for it.

On the way out of hospital I was photographed again, and the next day in the *Express & Star* 'before and after' photos appeared under the heading 'Machete heroine Lisa – I nearly lost an arm.' A reporter was there to interview me, and he also spoke to some of the hospital staff who described my recovery as 'miraculous, considering the severity of her injuries'. Pat Jones, the orthopaedic nurse manager, told him the speed of my recovery was amazing, and said, 'At the time it was a wonder she didn't lose her arm – it really was that bad.'

Spencer and I went out for lunch and then drove back to camp. I was so exhausted I fell asleep in the car. I arrived back at camp wearing the strap instead of the plaster and all the children wanted to see my arm. 'Let's have a look, Lisa,' they were saying, so I took my strap off for them. I was in great pain, but didn't want to show it. I wouldn't even take painkillers. The rest of the week was great fun, except for one incident. One night we heard police sirens nearby and I panicked. My chest felt like collapsing and I felt as if I was being strangled. I held on to my throat as if I was trying to loosen clothing to help me breathe. I felt so anxious and claustrophobic. There were too many things around me; I had to get free. Why were there police sirens? Was it all going to happen again? The feelings soon passed, but I wondered if this was the start of things to come. Was I going to feel like this more frequently? It was five weeks since the attack, but perhaps the shock was only just wearing off. It could be that because so many people had been around me I hadn't had time to think for those five weeks. Now reality was catching up with me.

The next morning the helpers told me there'd been some incident in the town, but they didn't elaborate. I felt that whatever had happened was worse than they were letting on; they were treading carefully with me. I was grateful for their concern, but I really wanted to be treated the same as anyone else. At least I was now back to normal after the fear of the night before. When I arrived home on Saturday, though, I went through another scene which was out of character for me. I only had a matter of hours to prepare for the USA trip, but I would usually have taken that in my stride. While Mum washed and dried my clothes and Nici helped me pack, I began to panic again. I said I didn't want to go to America and started to cry. I think part of the problem was the frustration of having to sit there while other people did everything for me.

At four the next morning, however, I was on the way to the airport, ready for the eight-hour first class flight to Orlando. At the airport I was recognised by so many people; I was starting to get used to it, but it was hard for Marc to cope with the fact that all those people felt they knew me. Once we got to our lovely hotel in Disney village we started to relax. It was so good to spend time alone with Marc after the hectic few weeks we'd been through. I couldn't do much and I felt worn out most of the time but it was still a great holiday. Marc was very concerned for me and did all he could to help. Apart from that we tried to behave as if the last few weeks hadn't happened. We didn't talk about the attack or anything connected with it; we were the same as we used to be together – as far as was possible. Nine days later we arrived home, feeling that the holiday had been an oasis in the desert and now we had to face media and public attention again.

It started the very next day, when I went to Ashley's seventh birthday party at the bowling ring. I couldn't bowl, of course, but watched Ashley and his friends, while perfect strangers kept coming up to talk to me. Most of them wanted to know how I was getting on, but others asked all sorts of questions like 'How big was his knife?' They weren't nasty, they just wanted to know. All week friends and family were still flocking to our house to visit me, and I had three visits to the hospital, again being recognised constantly. I hadn't made much progress with the movement in my fingers; it was frustrating that it was such a slow process. I was also continuing filming with BBC Midlands, who took me to St Luke's for one of the films. I had to stand outside the school and talk to the camera about how it felt to be standing there. It was so hard. All I could think about was flinging myself through the doors and children covered in blood. I'd had enough after that, and spent the rest of the day quietly.

But the following day, still only four days after returning from America, when I went into Wolverhampton for the first time since the attack, I had a dreadful experience. Nicola took me down there and at first we had a good time, apart from my constant awareness of the crowds of people around me. I discovered I'd developed a photographic memory. I could look behind me and glance at someone very briefly, then tell Nicola exactly what they looked like and what they were wearing. She'd turn round to check the details and I was right every time. It was rather frightening, but quite funny too. But then we were choosing a card in a shop, when I turned round and standing right behind me was a black man in a trilby hat. He looked like Horrett Campbell. He started to talk to me and Nicola; I think he might have been drunk. Suddenly I wasn't in the shop, I was in the playground at St Luke's. I saw the whole attack from beginning to end – the children's faces, the blood, the race to gather up the children. The scene ended with me in the ambulance. When at last I returned to the present, the man had gone and Nicola was saying, 'Are you all right, Lisa? Lisa?' I was shaking with fright. I told her what had happened and she took me for a coffee to calm me, before taking me home. I'd had my first flashback.

8 Flashbacks and Awards

In a way, that experience was more frightening than the day of the attack. On 8 July, as Horrett Campbell came running towards me wearing a trilby hat, I had no idea what to expect. That day in the shop I knew what could happen; what man was capable of. The next few weeks were bad in so many ways. That day in town seemed to mark the beginning of a period of fear and unhappiness, which wasn't helped by the start of a new school term.

Just a few days after my first flashback, the children were due to return to school, and I knew I wasn't physically able to go back with them. I was very unhappy about it, but decided I'd visit the school that day anyway. The *Express & Star* had called me to ask if I'd do a feature on Ahmed and Marium, as they prepared to return to school. They'd already checked it with their parents, who had agreed. So before school started I went to Ahmed and Marium's house. They saw me coming and ran down the path to hug me. I hadn't seen them for six weeks. It made me tearful, as they were as playful and happy as ever. The reporter asked their mum what she thought of me. Her English isn't brilliant, but she said, 'Words can't describe her. She saved Ahmed's life.' I thought, 'Gosh, did I really?' I felt touched, but quite embarrassed. I suppose I can't say

I *didn't* save his life – all right, I picked him up – but there's no halo round me.

I'd really wanted to go to school and see the children coming in, but both the school and the education department thought it was unwise because of the media attention. I cried so much to think they were going to school without me. When I arrived at occupational therapy later that morning, the press were there to ask how I felt about not being at school, and I managed to talk without breaking down. Later that afternoon, Mr Fallon picked me up to take me for a private visit to see the children. The press didn't know anything about it. It didn't feel the same as it would have if I'd been in school to welcome them back, but it was something. I didn't go into the nursery. All the children, except Ahmed, were now in the Reception class with the new teacher, Sarah Poole. They seemed settled, but it was weird to think they'd never again be enjoying themselves in the nursery. I broke down again when I got to bed that night. Looking back at my diary entry for 4 September I just wrote, 'Terrible day.'

The films I'd made with BBC Midlands were shown on three consecutive days, starting the day after term began. I reminded Marc to watch the films, but he said he didn't want to. He was finding it increasingly difficult to deal with all the publicity I was getting, and I had to accept that. It was so hard to keep everyone happy and balance everything – to include Marc, other friends and family, as well as go so often to hospital, see the psychologist and cope with the media, not to mention trying to understand what was going on in my own mind. But at least when I watched the films I was pleased with them and glad I'd done them. I felt I'd achieved something and the filming experience had been therapeutic. It had helped me get a lot out of my system.

Once the films had gone out I started receiving even more letters. They hadn't stopped coming, but now the flow increased. It was frustrating that my hand didn't allow me to reply to them all, although I wanted to. Flowers were still arriving and on average I had about twenty-five phone calls a day. I had a constant stream of visitors too, which cheered me up. What else was I to do when I couldn't go back to my job and I was still emotionally weak and physically unable to do much, including dress myself? The press attention hadn't died down either. I kept on doing interviews and photo shoots for national newspapers and magazines. The press would just turn up at the house, but most of them were polite and I thought I may as well do as they ask or they'll just keep on coming back.

I started to have nightmares about the attack from the week that term began. I'd wake terrified and drenched in sweat. Sometimes I felt too frightened to go to sleep at night, and tried to keep myself awake. I didn't tell anyone about it. I might occasionally say in the morning that I'd had a bad dream, but I didn't want to worry other people. Instead, I prayed a lot about it; I trusted God that these dreams wouldn't be with me for ever. Neither did I tell anyone that I woke up four or five times every night with an appalling throbbing pain in my arm. I might lie awake for half an hour before I could fall asleep again. There seemed no point in talking about it – who would it help? I didn't always smile, though; sometimes I'd talk to Mum and Pam about how I was feeling. They never seemed to tire of listening, but we'd always finish our conversations with a joke because that's how my family are, and to them I was still the same old Lisa.

The flashbacks were now more regular too. I'd be doing something ordinary like watching TV when suddenly I'd see the machete cutting across Francesca's face or Ahmed's head. I had another frightening experience, seeing a man wearing a trilby hat. He was walking along the pavement outside our house, and I was terrified. I saw him walk up the path to our front door, ready to kill us. It was a few seconds before I could acknowledge that he hadn't been anywhere near our door; he'd actually walked right past the house. I even knew the man – he lives further along our road. I knew I must get out of thinking like that; if I allowed myself to carry on, it might never leave me.

Pam had been with me that day; Mum had never left me alone in the house since the attack. If she had to go out, she always arranged for someone to sit with me. I managed to persuade her one day that I'd be all right by myself while she went shopping for an hour. But as soon as she went, I bolted all the doors and closed all the curtains upstairs and down. I sat there in the dark, panicking, longing for Mum's return. I was so frightened. What if Horrett Campbell had escaped and was coming to find me? That became a constant fear, which didn't leave me until after the court case. And the court case itself was also constantly at the back of my mind. I knew I would soon have to face Horrett Campbell and give evidence against him. As I discovered that day, one of the effects of the attack was that I hated to be alone indoors. Even now I can't settle to anything when I'm at home by myself. I usually have to get on the phone and start talking to someone.

There was one really happy event in among the sadness I was feeling at that time. In the middle of September I stayed for the weekend with Dawn, talked to her and had a good cry. She'd visited me every day without fail, cycling round with Ashley. That weekend she told me she was pregnant at last. I felt so bad that with all the things that had been happening to me I'd forgotten about Dawn's grief because she couldn't become pregnant. It was brilliant news and my tears for myself turned into tears of joy for Dawn and Terry. The warm, happy feeling that they were having a second baby at last brightened my days for the next few weeks.

I still wasn't going out socialising, but I went to my first Brownie meeting. I couldn't really do much with the children, but it was good to see them. I went to aerobics too, and again I couldn't take part properly, but I wanted to try to keep fit as much as possible. The previous January I'd started rehearsing for a dancing show which was to take place in Wolverhampton's Grand Theatre in March 1997. I'd had all this time off, but I was determined to be in it. So I went back to watch the others rehearsing and tried not to forget the steps. Apart from these outings, and trips to the hospital, I stayed in. It was so hard to sit at home when the children were back at school – that's where I should have been. There were some links with the school, though. The educational psychologist started coming to see me every month, keeping me updated with the children's progress. Some of the staff still came round or phoned, and Denise or Pam came often to bring letters and cards which had been delivered to me at St Luke's. I also began to visit the school regularly, although I didn't stay too long.

Progress seemed so slow, although reaching the next small stage was a big achievement. At occupational therapy Steve was funny and encouraging, keeping my spirits up. He rubbed cream into my scars and warmed up my hands, then I tried to grip and to pick things up. I had to squeeze a putty-like substance, which was so painful I sometimes screamed out. But no matter how hard I tried, I just hadn't the strength to move my wrist or make a fist. Another patient said to me one day, 'Doesn't it make you feel bitter that you have to go through all this because of what one man did in a few seconds?' I said it didn't, but on the way home I thought, 'Perhaps she's right.' Even so, I couldn't *feel* the bitterness. I still thought so much about what he did to the innocent children, that somehow I separated myself from them.

People asked, 'Do you forgive him?' I could easily forgive him for what he'd done to me, but not for what he did to the children. If he had killed us, at least I would have had twenty-one years of life, while they would only have had three or four. I have an amazing amount of love and support, and there are people out there who are so much worse off than me. How do the parents feel whose children were killed at Dunblane? I've got my life – that's something people forget when they wonder why I'm not bitter.

On the other hand, when I had bad days and people asked how I was, I sometimes wished I could say, 'I feel terrible today.' But I couldn't, because I didn't want to go into how I was feeling, I wanted to be normal. I felt as if all my emotions had been ripped out of me, stamped on, and put back in the wrong places. I was trying, without success, to fit them back in the right places, while at the same time dealing with the other demands on me. I smiled so much when I was interviewed on TV or photographed for the papers, and I must have given the impression that I was always happy. I was happy in one way, but behind the smile I sometimes suffered.

Those weeks after my first flashback were hard for me, although I don't think I actually became depressed. But from the middle of September so many things happened that I hadn't time to feel miserable. On 16 September I had a letter from Birmingham's *Evening Mail* to say I was one of their Diamond Award Winners – awards given for outstanding courageous or caring actions. All the winners were invited to a big luncheon at the Grand Hotel on 3 October. I thought it was so exciting. It was still only my second award, so I thought it was another one-off, like the Guides' award. It took a few more awards before I started to realise that the one-offs were beginning to mount into quite a pile.

A couple of days later a letter arrived from BBC Midlands, asking me if I would make a series of six films about where the money given the previous year to the Children in Need appeal had been spent. The five-minute films would be shown as part of the next Children in Need evening. I was glad that I was being offered something to keep me occupied, and it would be good experience, so I accepted. Soon after that I had a call from the *Express & Star*, inviting me to go with a reporter and photographer to the Association of British Editors conference in London. The conference was examining the media's response to major tragedies, and I was being asked to speak about how the press had dealt with me. Again, far from thinking I couldn't possibly do it, I was glad to have something to do.

A week later I made the first of the Children in Need films. I met Larry, the cameraman, again and really enjoyed myself, making films and friends and chatting with children. I enjoyed working on the films particularly because they weren't about the machete attack. Wherever I went, people made me feel so welcome. I visited a school in Wolverhampton where a girl had been given a wheel-chair as a result of the appeal. She was the most patient little girl, and when she said into the camera, 'Thank you to everyone who's given me this wheelchair,' I felt so moved. She was so much worse off than me. We also filmed at a riding school for the disabled, and a special school in Birmingham where money had been given to open a hydrotherapy pool. Sir Cliff Richard came to open the pool and I had the fantastic job of interviewing him. I was persuaded to get in the water, although I still had no feeling in my hand and I was embarrassed by the size of my thighs. I had to do ten takes because I kept messing it up – I had no idea they'd show those takes as part of the Children in Need programme.

At the end of September I had to break off filming for a few days because my diary was so full of other events. First I travelled down to London with a reporter and photographer from the *Express & Star*. I felt so worried when we arrived because of the noise and all the people; it was the first time I'd been in the capital since I was nine. That night I slept alone in a hotel room, and I had sickness and diarrhoea in the night through fright and fear of speaking in front of all those newspaper and television editors. In the end it wasn't too bad. I told the conference that the media had helped me through the ordeal, although my parents had been bombarded at home. A small section of journalists had used underhand means to get information about me, but on the whole I had been treated very well.

The next day I was at the Grand Hotel in Birmingham to receive my Diamond Award. Mum, Dad, Pam and Nicola came with me, and we were all so excited as we waited for a taxi to take us to Wolverhampton station. But just like the first time I'd got into a taxi after the attack, this driver was wearing a trilby hat. I panicked and said I couldn't get in. My family took me round the front of the car to look at his face. He looked nothing like Horrett Campbell, so I got in, but by then I was stressed and perspiring. At the hotel I met the other award-winners, including a nine-year-old leukaemia sufferer who had completed a motorbike ride from Land's End to John O'Groats with her dad, to raise money for other cancer victims, and a thirteen-year-old who had rescued two people from an ice-covered lake. I wondered what on earth I was doing there with all those people.

After lunch in the main ballroom came the award ceremony, where the presenter talked about each person, and I cried at every single one. Then we were called up individually to be presented with a diamond pin by jockey Bob Champion. I couldn't help realising that I was getting this award not because of some great sporting or acting achievement, but because of a quick decision I'd made to save children from an attacker. It was really hard to accept the award, knowing the trauma that lay behind it. Standing there, smiling, in front of lots of happy faces, I thought someone might run in to kill me. Perhaps it was because the day of the teddy bears' picnic was such a happy occasion, and I now knew terrible things could happen in the middle of the happiest scenes.

We'd been told one of the award-winners would be given the Super Diamond Award. As the presenter gave a big build-up to the final presentation, I looked round, wondering who deserved it most. I settled on the little girl with cancer, and I hoped it would be her. Suddenly the presenter was saying, 'Who better to get this award than the angel of St Luke's?' I just sat there, not moving. Mum nudged me: 'Lisa, go on, it's you.' Somehow I walked to the front, with a standing ovation going on all around me. It was like watching the Oscar ceremony on TV. I saw myself on the big screen at the front as I walked forward, and tried very hard to walk gracefully. In a way I couldn't understand what I was doing there. I had to let it all go over my head, and think it would be a good experience to tell my grandchildren about in the future.

But the presenter didn't give me the award. As I stood

there with him, he said, in his Midlands dialect, 'And who better to give you the award than the babies you saved?' The doors opened and in came Marium and Ahmed, with Emma Parlor and her brother Ben, dragging behind them a huge silver trophy with a diamond on the top. I had no idea they were there. It just about broke my heart. I could see everyone in the audience crying; it was so overwhelming. I kissed and hugged the children and told them how well they'd done. Marium said, 'Miss Potts, why are you crying?' and I said it was because I was so happy they were there.

After that I wasn't given a chance for another hour. I posed for photo after photo, gave countless interviews and received so many individual congratulations. When I was taken outside for photographs, I came face to face with a group of homeless people who were huddled outside the hotel. One shouted, 'What the hell have you got that for? You rich people always get these sparkling awards.' I felt guilty – perhaps he was right; I had just had a big meal in a posh hotel. But he was wrong about me being rich. I was only receiving my salary from the education department.

By the time the interviews were over, everyone else had gone home; there was only me, Mum, Dad, Pam and Nicola left. It had started to rain, and it took us ages to get home. I proudly placed the award on the fireplace next to the Guiding certificate. It still felt strange to watch myself on TV the next day, and to see myself on the front page of Birmingham's *Evening Mail*. I was still overwhelmed by it, still wondering what was happening to me. But I hadn't time to think, because that evening I was off again, this time to Derby, where I'd been invited to the Pann Union Conference, that's the union for nursery nurses. I stayed in a hotel by myself, and again felt afraid, particularly as I was still having terrible nightmares. On the way home on the train, a couple opposite me asked, 'Are you Lisa Potts?' and for the first time I felt like saying I wasn't. But of course I didn't, and we chatted for the rest of the journey. It was always good to listen to other people's stories of their lives.

The next week there was yet another award, and another the week after. I'd had a letter from the Guiding Commissioner inviting me to go to the Annual General Meeting in Codsall, but I didn't know why I was going there. It wasn't until I arrived that I discovered I was to be awarded the Silver Cross, the Guiding Association's highest award for courage, which is rarely presented. I think Mum and Dad were more proud of that than the Diamond Award. I was quoted in the paper the next day as saying, 'These awards are quite strange and unreal. I keep thinking, "Why me?" ' Within days I was in London again for a lunch with the editor of *Nursery World* magazine, and another presentation. I could take someone with me, so I asked Nicola. This time, instead of giving me an award, they presented me with a voucher for three nights for two people at a health farm. I could choose when to go, and in a couple of months' time, when things were getting out of hand for me, I would really appreciate it.

At last I heard that the children were getting an award too. Going into school the day after the Diamond Award ceremony, I'd been met by Francesca, who told me that she, Reena and Ahmed had been interviewed and photographed by the Birmingham *Sunday Mercury*. They were going to receive Wonderkids awards at a ceremony later in the year, and all three of them were so excited. It was a joy to see their happy, smiling faces in the paper that weekend, under the heading, 'We honour the bravest tots in the Midlands.'

I'd been lifted out of my earlier unhappiness by all these

events, but the reality of the flashbacks, nightmares, constant pain and slow progress was with me all the time. I had learnt to write by now, so could reply to a few of the many letters, but each one took so long. I *longed* to drive, but wasn't allowed to. But I did have a lovely coach trip and day out at a safari park with all the children who had been involved in the attack. It had been paid for by the *Express & Star* and West Midlands Travel, because the children had missed the trip they should have had the week after the attack. We were going to have a picnic, so it was a worrying time for us all – the first picnic together since 8 July. Taishion asked me, 'Will the man with the machete be there?' I told him this would be a really happy picnic, but he still asked, 'Are you sure?' Francesca thought it was funny that we both had to rub cream on our scars, and asked to look at mine. She asked many questions: 'Can I look at what the man did to you? Have you seen my face? Do you feel sad sometimes?' We had formed a bond because of what we had been through together. We chatted that day about the events of the attack. I never asked them about it; I always waited for them to talk to me first. It was a healing experience for us to go on that trip together. Of course the whole thing was in the *Express & Star* the next day, but I was so pleased to see Nicola on the front page instead of me. I was very conscious of getting all the attention and being in the paper so often; I was sure people must be getting fed up with me. People would stop me in the street and say, 'In the paper again today, Lisa?' and I'd say I was sure it wouldn't be for much longer.

I felt the same about Linda, the temporary Reception teacher at the time of the attack. She'd suffered too, and she had to deal with her own feelings about holding the door shut against Horrett Campbell – and against me – but she wasn't getting media attention. We started to see each other regularly, and talked a lot about the attack. I think Mum, Pam and Marc thought I didn't talk to them enough, but it was easier to talk to someone who'd been there. We also talked about how it would be in court, because by this time we'd both received an order to attend the trial of Horrett Irvine Campbell at Stafford Crown Court.

There were still a few weeks to go before the trial, though, and Mum asked me to go with her and Pam to Turkey during October half-term. I didn't want to be away from home for a whole week. I felt insecure and frightened about being away from the many people with whom I'd become so close in the past months. But I went and, although I still had nightmares and flashbacks, it was a break to be away from everything. I gathered my thoughts, and began to write down how I felt.

I needed to gather my energy, because when I came back there was another round of public appearances within one week. Local firemen invited me to light the bonfire in Bilston on 1 November. I was treated like a VIP when I got there and, yet again, I appeared in the local paper the next day. The next two occasions were rather more spectacular. Before I'd gone to Turkey I had two letters. The first told me I'd been awarded a Celebrities Guild Unsung Hero Award and was invited to an awards dinner at the Dorchester Hotel in London on 3 November. The second was from The Royal Association for Disability and Rehabilitation to tell me I had won a Radar Abbey National People of the Year Award, to be presented at London's Park Lane Hilton Hotel on 6 November.

Marc came with me to the Dorchester. He wore a dinner suit, and I wore a new dress which Linda had bought for me, 'because of all that's happened', she said. It was a glorious, fantastic evening, attended by famous people like Jeremy Irons, Lenny Henry and Stirling Moss. I didn't feel in awe of them – they're only human like everyone else – and I was starting to get a feel of how they felt to be on public show. The award, a glass bowl, was presented by Jill Dando, and the organisation's tribute was that I 'loved children and suffered for them'.

Mixing with the rich and famous has its funny side. I was talking to people beforehand, when one lady noticed my Gucci watch, which was, in fact, a cheap fake.

'Oh *darling*, what a super watch!' she said 'Is it a seven two five, eight two five or nine two five?'

I had no idea what she was talking about, so I had to say, 'What do you mean?'

'Money, sweetie, money,' she said.

'Oh, no, it was a fiver from Turkey,' I told her. I don't know who was more embarrassed, me or her.

I tried to encourage Marc, but he found the whole evening very difficult. Going home on the train the next day we had a long talk about everything. The last few months had been so hard for us. I'd been going out with him since I was sixteen, and we were good friends who knew each other so well, but the thing that had happened to me had turned my life upside down. I was living a different life – and not by choice – while Marc was still the same. We couldn't do all the things we used to; we couldn't even walk down the street together without people stopping to talk to me. I so much wanted Marc to fit in to my new life, but he couldn't, particularly as he is such a quiet person. I was finding it hard to relate to him, and all my emotions were so mixed up. Before the train had arrived in Wolverhampton, we had decided it would be best for us both if we split up. I wanted us to stay as friends, but we thought it best not to see each other for a short time.

I loved Marc dearly and still do, and I couldn't blame

him for not enjoying what was going on. But I never thought this would happen and I was heartbroken. Two days later, at dawn, Marc and I were supposed to be catching a train to take us back to London, this time to the Park Lane Hilton. I asked Marc if he could come with me for just one more ceremony, but he said he couldn't face it all again. How could I possibly go to the People of the Year Award Ceremony now? How could I face the cameras, the reporters, or being on a public platform and looking as if I was enjoying myself? On the other hand, I'd accepted the invitation, so how could I *not* go? The media would eventually find out why I wasn't at such an important occasion, and there would be so much fuss about me and Marc. I was distraught, but I forced myself to go. At the last minute my cousin Dominic agreed to come with me in Marc's place.

I put on a brave face but inside I was hurting so much. Travelling down on the train, only thirty-six hours after Marc and I had split up, I considered the way my life had turned upside down. Things were moving in a way I'd never imagined. I knew I couldn't go back to being the person I was before the attack and I had to learn to accept that. Yet I felt like the same old me, and my friends kept telling me I hadn't changed. That meant a lot to me.

I was already feeling emotional when I arrived at the Park Lane Hilton, so when I was introduced to Ron Taylor, headmaster of Dunblane Primary School, I couldn't help crying. We talked a lot about what had happened in our schools, and had to be interviewed and photographed again and again. Ron Taylor was given his award for the 'dignity and humanity' he showed following the Dunblane massacre, but in an interview he said, 'I don't see it as an award at all. I see it as a recognition for all the staff in Dunblane who have worked very, very hard for the past few months to try to re-establish some semblance of normality and as effective a teaching and learning environment for the kids as possible.' I wanted to say something like that, but the papers just reported that I 'expressed surprise at being singled out from the school's staff for the award'. But I'm glad one paper quoted me as saying of Ron Taylor, 'He is a remarkable man who has handled himself with great dignity and strength. I felt like I wasn't worthy of being nominated alongside him.'

The fourteen award-winners, in several different categories, included cricket umpire Dickie Bird and Olympic rowing gold medallist Steven Redgrave. There was a fanfare of trumpets as we each walked in to collect our award. Everyone stood and clapped when it was my turn, and although I was crying inside, I was smiling cheerfully on the photos in next day's press. Nobody knew what was going on inside me that day, and there was still more to come after the ceremony. I had agreed to take part in some filming later in London for a BBC documentary, *Reasons to Remember*, which was about the awards I'd been given. I'd been filmed at the awards ceremony, and then the crew came to Wolverhampton to film me with the children. They also followed me through the streets to film all the people who came to talk to me as I walked along.

By that time, people who met me in the street often asked, 'Are you over it now?' They were asking that question at the same time as I'd started to feel it had only just begun. It was four months since the attack, but in a sense it felt like one week. On the other hand, I felt like a much older person. And although I seemed so chatty and cheerful, going into town was still an ordeal. One day, shortly after the awards, I panicked so much that I had to go home. There were so many people there, and it seemed as if half of them were stopping to talk to me. I was still 'playing the game' of memory skills, knowing exactly what people behind me were wearing after only a brief glance. It was unnerving at the best of times, but on this particular day it was so packed with people that I couldn't even *see* who was behind me – they were so close that they were pushing against me. That night I had a terrible nightmare; Ahmed's head had been cut right open and he had died, and I was at his funeral. I woke up crying and sweating, and had to go into school the next day to make sure everyone was all right.

The public and the media didn't know this hidden side of me, though, and the very next day I was in full swing for the week of Children in Need. I was busy with the preparations for the whole week. In just one day I was at the hospital for occupational therapy in the morning, went straight on to Birmingham to do a press call at *Pebble Mill* with Toby Anstis and Diane Youdale (Jet from *Gladiators*), then to the *Midlands Today* studios to do a live interview with Sue Beardsmore and to be photographed with Pudsey Bear. I had to go back to Wolverhampton by taxi to be ready for aerobics in the evening. Why I insisted on going to aerobics after a day like that, I don't know. On the night Children in Need was broadcast, I appeared live to present all of my six films. Some of my old teachers from Smestow were in the audience. One of them said afterwards, 'I can't believe all that's happened to you,' and I replied, 'Nor me, to be honest – I can't believe I'm here on live television.'

I enjoyed making new friends and many of the new experiences I was having. Through working on Children in Need I met the people from the BBC *Style Challenge* programme, and I asked them if I could go on with Mum. A researcher came round to talk about it, and we were booked to appear at the end of November. Mum was so nervous – I think she wished I hadn't asked – but it was a brilliant day. It was nice for Mum really – she'd been a bit forgotten, after all she'd done for me – and we came away with free clothes. At the end of the programme Francesca, Reena and some other children came on. When the designers saw them they were so moved they had to go off the screen. The hairdressers had put a blue streak in my hair, which shocked Reena. 'Miss Potts, why have they painted your hair?' she said. I used to wonder what on earth these children thought I was doing, popping up on TV and in the papers so often.

The court case, which I'd successfully kept at the back of my mind, was nearly upon me. I'd been summoned to appear on Monday 2 December 1996. Carol Bucknall, the CID officer who had taken over from Jean, had been to see me often in the two months before court. The Friday before the case began, she took me, Dorothy Hawes and Philippa Parlor to a court in Wolverhampton so we could see what would happen. She showed us round, explained where we'd stand and talked us through the procedure. Dorothy and Philippa were both nervous, but I wasn't. I couldn't understand why not; I think I expected to take it all in my stride. And I still had a whole weekend to go.

I tried to have a normal weekend: dancing, aerobics, crèche and Christmas shopping. By Sunday evening I was beginning to feel quite tense. Then the phone rang; Carol was phoning to say the case had been postponed until Wednesday. I felt relieved that I could put it off for another two days. But, of course, those two days went only too fast, and I was in bed by 10.30 on the Tuesday night. I didn't usually go until at least midnight. I was only a little bit nervous, but when I woke on the Wednesday morning I felt terribly sick. Carol and Andy, another CID officer, came to collect me at 8.30. Mum, Dad and Pam followed us in Pam's car – and Marc followed in his. Marc and I hadn't wanted our relationship to end with us not talking to each other, and we remained good friends. He had been such a huge part of my life, so I was very happy that he had chosen to come to court to support me.

All the way to Stafford I was asking Carol and Andy about Horrett Campbell and how he'd been behaving in prison, but of course they couldn't tell me much. They were consoling me constantly. The journey went so quickly, although it's eighteen miles. As we drove past the court to the car park beyond, all I could see were photographers and cameramen. I remember saying to myself, 'I'll get through this – I've got to – and before I know it, it will be all over.' It seemed a long walk from the car park to the court, but Carol and Andy were wonderful, making jokes and keeping cheerful as we walked along together. And all the time the cameras were flashing, and people were walking backwards in front of me, filming as they went. But I'd got to know so many of the press over the last five months, and when they called, 'Hello Lisa, are you all right?' and 'Best of luck, Lisa, you'll be OK,' I felt they were supporting me as much as anyone.

I was taken into the room where I had to wait, and was glad when Mum, Dad, Pam and Marc were shown in too. Someone brought us coffee, and I talked to Marc. Denise arrived with her daughter, then Linda and her daughter. I hugged Linda and talked to her for a while. I'd had that lost feeling again; I was in my world, apart from everyone else, but somehow I felt Linda was in that world with me. Perhaps it was because we were both to give evidence.

Everyone except those who were giving evidence had to go into court and take their seats in the balcony. Then we just had to wait – and the waiting was awful. We went into the next room to see Dorothy Hawes, Philippa and Wendy. I felt claustrophobic; the room was far too small for all of us. Linda suggested we went to the cafeteria for more coffee. Carol gave us our statements to read. I kept looking at my watch, wondering when I was going to be called – although looking at my watch didn't help, as there couldn't be a time given for each person. Neither Linda nor I had eaten that day, but we couldn't seem to stop drinking coffee. Larry, the BBC cameraman, came in to the cafeteria. He said to Carol, 'I know I'm not allowed to talk to Lisa, but can I give her a hug?' I kept looking at the clock and asking Carol, 'When will it be?' but, of course, she had no more idea than I had. By 11.30, when I asked her for the umpteenth time, she said, 'It will probably be after lunch now.'

She was right. Mum, Dad, Pam, Marc and Denise came down to the cafeteria for lunch, but they weren't allowed to talk to us. It was weird to be sitting at another table, in the same room as my family, and not to make any contact with them. It was also frustrating to think that they'd spent the morning in court, and they knew all that had gone on, while we knew nothing. I longed to go over and hug Mum, and to be told everything that had happened in court. Linda and I tried to eat, but we couldn't manage much. I had a constant dragging pain in my left hand and arm – much worse than usual.

Just before each person was called to give evidence they had to go to a room upstairs. After lunch, Carol said it was time to go up. My nerves, already frayed, started to jangle. As we got upstairs I saw Dorothy, just about to walk into court. I asked if she was all right, and she nodded. I thought, 'It's going to be me in a minute.' I sat with Philippa Parlor and tried to talk, but it was Carol who kept the conversation going. I drank more black coffee. Then Sheila, who'd been helping at the nursery that day, was called into court. I was brought into the passageway to wait. The press were scribbling away, some of them saying, when they saw me, 'All right, Lisa?' Most of the faces I recognised. There were so many people around, walking up and down. My stomach was churning. I started to sweat badly, and had to take my jacket off. Just when I thought I couldn't stand it any more, I heard a voice call, 'Lisa Potts!' Carol gave me a big hug and said, 'You'll be all right. We'll be sitting at the back.' The courtroom door opened to admit me. I turned round as I was walking in and saw all the press crowding in behind me.

9 *The Witness Stand*

I was led to the witness stand. As I walked forward, I thought, 'Gosh, this is me, at the age of twenty-two, going into a courtroom to give evidence against a man charged with attempted murder.' I wanted to have a good look round before I started giving evidence. First I looked up to the balcony and saw my family and Marc. Opposite me were the jury, and to my left, the judge. He had such a kind face, and I warmed to him straight away. The press were packed in behind me. The prosecuting counsel and defence counsel were to my right. Behind them, I knew, was Horrett Campbell. I didn't want to look at him properly until after I'd given evidence, but I just had to see him before it all began. I braced myself, then very quickly turned my head to the right and gave him the briefest glance. What I saw didn't fit my image of the man who'd attacked me. This man was sitting behind a plastic screen in the dock and he seemed so small. This surely wasn't the huge man who had attacked me with the machete? And yet I knew it was.

I had no more time to think, because I had to swear the oath. Then I prayed a quick prayer, 'Please, Lord, help me stay calm and not panic through all this.' From then on I must have been the calmest person in the court. I had such a sense of peace for the hour and ten minutes I was giving evidence. I was asked if I wanted to sit or stand, and I chose to stand. I thought, 'I've looked at Horrett Campbell, I won't look at him again, I'll look at the jury.' There was no expression on their faces at all.

The prosecuting counsel, Mr Richard Wakerley QC, began to ask me details about the day of the attack. He asked me about the scene in the nursery playground before Horrett Campbell appeared, exactly when he came running in, and how he jumped the fence. I answered him so calmly, describing it as I had so many times before.

Then came a question I wasn't expecting: 'Do you think it will upset you to hold the machete?' Throughout the questions and answers, I had heard the noise of the pens behind me scratching away. Now they stopped. There was complete silence as the court waited for my answer.

I looked straight at the jury and said, 'I don't think it will upset me.' The moment of tension had passed and the press picked up their pens again.

The court usher gave me a plastic glove to put on, and then he held out the machete. It was a dirty, bloodstained knife with a big wooden handle and a blade sixteen inches long. There was a gasp around the court as I took it in my hand. I stared at it. There were words inscribed on it which I couldn't see properly, but I managed to make out 'You filthy devils' and '666 marks the Beast'. I knew I had to look at Horrett Campbell again. I wondered how he felt when he saw me holding his machete. I glanced to my right and saw him leaning forward with his face pressed right up against the screen, staring at me. I felt sick. I looked back at the tip of the blade and suddenly, like a flash, I saw Francesca's face being ripped open. But somehow my calmness didn't leave me, and when Mr Wakerley said, 'Miss Potts, would you like to show the jury how Horrett Campbell struck you and the children with the machete?' I thought, 'I'm going to show them exactly how he did it; they need to know.'

I lifted the knife right above my head, brought it straight down, and said, 'That's how he did it, but it came down with great force.' As I spoke, I looked at the jury, and then at the judge, because I'd been told to speak to everybody.

I didn't have any time to think about how I felt about using the knife, because it was being taken from me and the next question was coming along. But as I handed it back to the usher, I glanced at the blade and again saw it cutting through Francesca's face, this time played out in slow motion. I had to close my eyes for a second and tell myself, 'I'm in court, I have to give my account and think straight.' I prayed again, and still felt peaceful.

More questions came, which all seem a blur as I look back. Then Mr Wakerley needed to know exactly where the children were in relation to me, and he gave me photographs of the nursery to look at. They were in a booklet, labelled A, B, C, and so on. I was asked to explain, for example, where Ahmed was and where I was on picture E. As I turned the pages I saw this place which was covered in blood; it was splattered everywhere. I thought, This isn't the nursery I was in. I'd never seen it looking like that before. The nursery had been the bright place where I'd worked and the children had played, but these were photographs of a war zone. It wasn't St Luke's School, it wasn't real life; it was a television programme. But I knew it *was* St Luke's School, and I was standing in court having to talk about where the children had been in these pictures. I gave my answers, still calm despite the shocks that were being handed out to me; then Mr Wakerley thanked me and sat down.

It was the turn of the defence counsel, Mr Ian Peddie QC. The first thing he asked me was, 'Is this your statement?' and I was given the paper that I'd signed in hospital after the attack. He asked, 'Did you sign the bottom of this?'

I started to feel nervous, thinking I must be on trial, but then thought perhaps he had to ask me this because he didn't think it looked like a signature. So I explained, 'Yes, but both my hands were in traction at the time.'

I prayed again, and said to myself, 'Come on, stay calm.' He wanted me to look at the nursery photographs again, and we went through exactly where I was when my five knife blows were inflicted, and how I was holding my hands at the time. I think he was trying to prove that Horrett Campbell didn't actually come in to the nursery.

'Surely, with all those children screaming and you in shock, you couldn't be sure he went into that little passageway?'

I thought, 'Yes, of course he did, I was there!' But it was only me versus him – the children couldn't be called to give evidence. It was so frustrating. I *knew* he had been in there, and had been hitting me on the back at the time. I could see it all in my mind.

Mr Peddie asked me to look at one particular picture, and he asked where it had been taken. I told him it was the Reception class. He asked me what I saw on the floor of the Reception class.

'The sheath of the knife with blood around it,' I replied.

'How did it get there?'

'I don't know.' How could I know? To this day I have no idea how the sheath could have found its way into a room Horrett Campbell hadn't even been in.

He then held up a hat with a strap underneath it and asked if it was the one Horrett Campbell had been wearing. I knew it was – this was the thing that had been giving me more flashbacks than anything else.

'Yes, that's the hat he wore,' I replied.

He asked me several more questions, about the bag Campbell was carrying, and where exactly he jumped the wall. Then he said, 'Thank you very much,' and sat down.

It was all over. But not quite – there was something else. The Judge, Mr Justice Sedley, had something to say which, I found out afterwards, was unusual before the end of a trial. 'Your conduct was very brave indeed,' he told me. 'I am sure you would say it was no more than any teacher or nursery nurse would have done. You acted with great unselfishness. You are a credit to your profession. I want that fact to be acknowledged.'

Could this man really be saying those words to me? It felt as if he was talking to someone else called Lisa Potts, who must be sitting behind me. I suddenly felt that lost sensation again, but at the same time I had a warm feeling. I felt as I had done at school when I'd been praised, as if I was special, and happy at the words that were spoken to me – but this time it was so different. Tears came to my eyes, but I said to myself, 'No, Lisa, hold them back.'

As I left the court I wanted to look at Horrett Campbell for a long time, but I had to keep walking. But I did look at him quickly, and I felt so sorry for him. This man had done so much damage to us – not just to me and the children, but to our parents, families, the whole school, the wider community. He'd affected us all through his actions. I felt sorry that he could do such a thing; he must have been so ill to have done it. I've felt sorry for him ever since.

There was a break in the proceedings, and Carol took me for yet another coffee. As we walked towards the cafeteria, she told me I'd been fantastic, and said Mr Wakerley wanted a short word with me. He approached me and said, 'In all my years as a QC, I have never heard anyone speak with such calmness. You are a very exceptional person.' It touched me so much, and I couldn't keep my public face on for any longer. I went into the toilet and broke down. Two wonderful things had been said to me in the midst of such an awful court case. One minute I was faced with evil, with a man who nearly killed me, who engraved the numbers '666' on his knife; the next minute I was being told I was an exceptional person. I felt so confused.

When I returned to Carol, we went up to the balcony in the courtroom, ready to see the rest of the trial. It was so lovely to join the family up there, now my ordeal was over. Mum hugged me, and Denise took my hand and said I'd done so well. Then we heard the words 'Court rise' and the court was in session again. I sat back in my chair, thinking, 'Good luck, Linda.' I hadn't heard Dorothy, Sheila, Wendy or Reena's mum give evidence, and hadn't been allowed to see them afterwards, so this was the first time I'd been an observer. As I watched Linda walk to the witness stand, I felt frightened for her, and thought, 'She's so brave, to stand up there.' It was as if I hadn't been there myself only minutes before. I tried to tell myself, 'That was me, standing there, being sworn in, answering questions,' but it didn't seem real.

Linda was superb. Her version of events came from a different perspective. She'd been working in the Reception class when she'd looked up and seen Horrett Campbell through the window. She'd been the one to drag in Wendy, whose head was bleeding, and it was Linda who shouted to Denise to call the police. She took responsibility for Francesca after she'd been attacked. She spoke of holding on to the Reception door to protect the twenty-five children in her class from Campbell, even though she could see me on the other side of the door. I felt very sad for her, realising again what a terrible dilemma it must have been for her. She was so brave to have held on to that door handle. She felt guilty, but it was so much better to do what she did, and to save another whole class of children. What's my life compared to the lives of twenty-five children? And then she said she'd seen Campbell attacking me on the back as I stood in that small area outside the Reception door, and it made me feel so much better that someone else had confirmed my story. I heard Denise say under her breath, 'Well done, Linda.'

When Linda's evidence was finished, I couldn't wait for her to come upstairs so I could tell her how brilliant she'd been. It was nearly time to finish for the day, and I was so relieved that I'd given my evidence and didn't have to go back to court if I didn't want to. But I did want to. I wanted to see the whole thing through from beginning to end, so Carol and Andy said they'd continue to pick me up each morning. They were both so good to me, constantly making sure I was all right and could cope.

Once I got home, I was able to read in the *Express & Star* all the details I'd missed from the morning's proceedings. Mr Wakerley had told the jury that Campbell was pleading 'Not guilty' to attempted murder, but admitting the lesser charges of causing grievous bodily harm with intent and one charge of attempting to cause grievous bodily harm. Campbell had gone to the school with a bag containing the machete, a knife, a bottle full of petrol and two iron bars with sponges on the top. I found it almost unbelievable that he not only went to attack us, but also wanted to set the school on fire. He had thought about the attack for up to a month before, and in police interviews had said he thought the school had turned against him 'because young children had jeered at him when he walked past'. 'I just wanted to hurt them,' Campbell had told police. 'I thought I would hurt them pretty badly, depending where they were hit.' After the attack, Campbell returned to Villiers House where he started two small fires, then ran to the roof to watch police activity at the school below him. Mr Wakerley told the jury, 'He admits he was there and that he intended to cause grievous bodily harm. The issue for you is whether he intended to kill.'

I felt quite stunned as I read the words and, as I had when I'd read the paper in hospital, I had to sit for a long time and consider the words 'attempted murder' and 'intended to kill'. Somehow my mind couldn't fully grasp the implications of the words. I tried to tell myself that this man could have killed me. Instead of standing up in court, testifying against him, I could quite easily have been dead. Not alive, not breathing, not here any more – because of this man.

I was stunned too, although in a different way, when I read what Mr Wakerley had said to the jury about me: 'You may well be astonished by the courage of that young girl, as she could so easily have shut that door, gone further inside to find help, gone to her headmistress. But for her action this tragedy could have been so much worse.'

I hardly slept that night, or any other night while the court case continued. I didn't want to eat much, either. All the days seemed condensed into one whole day; when we arrived at court in the morning, it was as if we hadn't been home and gone to bed. There everyone was again, the judge in his wig and gown, Horrett Campbell in the dock, just as they had been the day before. As usual, I was photographed going in, and photographed going out, but none of the press could speak to me until after the case.

Philippa Parlor gave evidence in the morning. She described Horrett Campbell bringing the knife down 'as you would cutting corn', and said the children were running around 'like chickens in a pen'.

'He came towards us and brought the machete up above my daughter Emma,' she told the jury. 'If I had not thrown her sideways he would have hit her. I am sure of that.'

She described how she grabbed her own two children and another child, and ran into the toy shed. She shut the door and held on to it, unable to lock it because the key was on the other side. There were two very hard pulls on the door, which could not have come from a child, she said. She stayed in the shed, even after it had gone quiet outside, and she thought he had killed everybody. Then a man came to the door and kept telling her it was all right to come out.

Then it was Andy's turn to give evidence. 'Detective Constable Andrew Barnsley' was called, and he told the jury the details of the police interviews with Campbell. I was amazed to hear that he had described himself as a 'normal sort of person, kind, considerate and sensitive'. He had got out of bed after midday on 8 July and later 'went to the school to attack some people'. Andy seemed to be speaking for hours, and all that he said was borne out the next day when Horrett Campbell was called to the witness stand by the defence. As he walked forward, I leaned over the balcony to get a good look at this man. I wasn't frightened at that stage, but I was very keen to hear him speak. As he swore the oath and I heard him for the first time, I was surprised. I had been expecting a deep, aggressive voice, but his voice wasn't aggressive at all. He was hesitant, pausing after he was asked questions, and he tended to mumble. At times he seemed confused, skipping from one answer to another. He came across as mentally ill, but at the same time he seemed intelligent.

As he gave his evidence I started to sweat and my heart

began to race. I felt trapped as I focused on this man, seeing him as a blurred image. I kept asking myself, 'Why did he do it?' I couldn't understand. He was given a piece of rolled-up paper with which to demonstrate how he attacked his victims. The defence counsel said he only struck once at five of his victims, and asked him why he struck Lisa Potts more than once. He answered, 'I did not feel the machete was making any contact with her. I sort of brushed her with it. I did not think I had really hit her. I would have stopped once I knew the blade had made contact.' I felt very cold and physically sick. These people were discussing my life. He had hit the others only once, he said, because they were not the only ones to take the blame. He was being persecuted by the whole community, and he had to hurt them. He said it wasn't his intention to kill – if it had been, he would have hit harder with the machete. Asked if he could have killed if he'd wanted to, Campbell answered, 'Probably, yes.'

I wanted to leave court then. It was so disturbing that he was talking about attacking me and the children. I felt trapped and claustrophobic, and wanted to run out into the biggest field I could find. At the same time I felt I needed to listen, because for the rest of my life I would always want to know what this man said.

He was being asked if he believed the attack was evil. He answered, 'What I did was good.' I didn't hate him for saying that, because I knew he was ill. He was asked to put on the hat he wore, with two screws in it, which the prosecution said represented horns. As he put on the hat, he suddenly became the man who hit me. I slipped down in my chair, shaking. It *was* him. For the first time I could actually see that man attacking *me*. Always before that I had had flashbacks or nightmares of him attacking the children. Now I saw him running towards me; I saw the ugly grimace on his face. I saw myself raising my hands to protect my face as he lifted the machete. The feeling of total panic came back. I was terrified. Mum and Andy, on each side of me, asked if I wanted to go out, but I said I needed to listen to a bit more.

Campbell said he thought the children and mothers he attacked were filthy people and represented the devil. He felt sorry for himself after the attack, but not for his victims. When asked why he used a machete rather than a penknife or stick, he said it was because it 'suited his purpose'. I had to leave then. I couldn't stand it any more. I was having constant flashbacks, which played over and over again in my head as I looked at Campbell. Andy and I crept out round the side and went to have coffee. I was shaking so badly and felt as if I was going to be sick. After about twenty minutes I managed to tell myself that I'd come to court to hear this man and I must see it through. When we walked back in, he was talking about hearing voices which had insulted him for five years. It wore him down and there was nothing he could do to stop it. 'There was a conspiracy against me and just about everybody was involved. I felt I had to get even. I felt victimised. I think I was missing out on things and everyone seemed to be in my business. They knew what I was doing and every move that I made.'

He described the day of the attack, when he had walked to the school the long way round, going through the church gate. At the side of the school he had taken the machete out of his bag and left the sheath in there. I remembered looking at the photograph of the sheath in the Reception classroom and being asked how it got there, and to this day I don't suppose anyone knows. Campbell heard a girl in the school grounds say, 'If he does it, then he does it.' He thought the girl must know why he was there, and she would think it funny if he didn't go on. He then had no option, he said, but to carry out the attack. I wondered who this girl was – perhaps it was the voice he was hearing inside his head.

I was exhausted by the time Campbell's evidence came to an end, but there was more to come. The psychiatrist who had been treating Campbell said he had paranoid schizophrenia but didn't know it. He said Campbell had probably been suffering with the condition for several years, and that he was still capable of forming an intent to do something, such as to kill.

Then it was time for the closing speeches. Mr Wakerley told the jury that when Campbell attacked his victims the issue was, 'did he intend to kill them?' Campbell had planned his attack, chosen the machete and written on the blade. 'What, simply, can a man like that intend but to kill?' asked Mr Wakerley.

But for the defence, Mr Peddie asked the jury to accept that Campbell was the victim of paranoid schizophrenia, who reacted as he did 'because he wanted desperately to stop the abuse he believed he was hearing'. Campbell's evidence to police and in court showed that he went to the school to hurt, not to kill. Campbell had shown courage, said Mr Peddie, in pleading guilty to the lesser charges of wounding, and in giving evidence in the witness box.

When proceedings came to a close I felt completely lost and drained. I felt so alone, and unable to express to anyone how I felt. I wanted to sit by myself for the whole weekend, going over all that had been said during the past three days. Hearing Horrett Campbell's voice for the first time, seeing him properly as he gave evidence, and hearing what he had to say, had shaken me. It was one of the most miserable weekends of my life. I wasn't in a hurry for Monday to come so that I could hear the verdict, but by the time I got to court on the Monday morning, I just wanted it all over and done with. I sat in the balcony with Denise, Linda and Francesca's family who had come to hear the verdict, as well as Carol and Andy, as the judge summed up. Then the jury went out, and it was a case of waiting. We had to wait three hours before they came back.

Each charge of attempted murder was dealt with separately, and the foreman was asked if the jury found Horrett Campbell guilty or not guilty of attempted murder. In every case she answered, 'Guilty.' I heard people saying 'Yes!' under their breath. There seemed to be a feeling of release for everyone else, but I felt absolutely nothing. I was numb – no happiness or sadness; I felt completely flat. I wanted to feel something but I didn't. I'd expected to feel so happy – and yes, I did feel the sentence was good and right. But for those final minutes of the court case, my only discernible feeling was relief that it was all over, and I could now get on with my life.

I heard Mr Justice Sedley adjourn sentencing for another three months, and remand Campbell to Ashworth Hospital, a maximum security psychiatric unit on Merseyside. He warned Campbell to be under no illusions as to his ultimate fate. To my amazement, he then told the jury he would be recommending me for a bravery award. 'You may well be thinking that Lisa Potts deserves more formal recognition. I think so, too. I shall be taking what steps I can to ensure that is considered.'

As we stood for the judge to go out, I wanted to smile at the jury, even to reach out and hug them all. When we went downstairs, everyone was so pleased with the verdict, and I was pleased too, but I couldn't seem to feel much except that lost feeling. I knew I had to pull myself together because I had to go out and face the media, who hadn't been allowed to talk to me for almost a week. There were at least fifty of them waiting out there and it seemed it was me they wanted. All around me people were saying, 'Rather you than me – but go on, Lisa, you'll be all right.'

I thought, 'I've been through so much already, I can handle this.' I walked out and was immediately surrounded. Microphones were pushed under my nose and question after question was fired at me: 'How do you feel now it's all over?' 'What do you think of the sentence?' 'How did it feel to hold the machete?' 'How did you feel about facing Horrett Campbell?' 'When are you going back to school?'

I told myself to keep calm, and told the press I felt relieved that it was over, that I was glad to have been shown the machete, that it was frightening but had helped me to see Campbell in the witness box, that I was going back to school in the New Year. I told them I was certain Campbell had been trying to kill me – I had seen it clearly in his eyes. I couldn't begrudge the media; I knew they had a job to do and that the public wanted to know the answers to all the questions they were asking me. I gave them all they wanted, and eventually they thanked me and went.

At last Carol and Andy took me off in the car. All I wanted to do was go home for a rest, but the police had invited me to the CID Christmas party. At least, I thought, when I got home at four o'clock that afternoon, I'd have four hours rest before I went out again. But even that was denied me. The phone never stopped; GMTV and Sky *Breakfast News* both phoned to arrange live interviews for the next morning; magazines and papers phoned to arrange to meet me or to interview me over the phone. I was handling all the calls, and trying to make notes in between so I wouldn't forget the times and dates of all the appointments. I didn't have time to sit down or to think at all before Carol collected me that evening. Even at the party I was called out three times to reception to take calls. It was a good party, though, and I didn't get back until the early hours of the next morning. Unfortunately, I had to be up at six o'clock to prepare for the breakfast television interviews.

10 Difficult Times

There was no danger of oversleeping anyway. At six
o'clock I was woken by the sound of buzzing in the street;
the crews were already setting up. I should think it woke
most of the neighbours too. When everything was ready, I
talked first to Anthea Turner on GMTV, then to Sky *News*.
As soon as I'd finished, more photographers and journalists
were knocking on the door. The whole afternoon was taken
up with filming for the BBC programme *Here and Now*,
which involved talking about the court case, meeting the
children in their homes, and walking about in town. While
I was out, Mum took no less than forty messages for me at
home. My mobile phone didn't stop ringing either. I'd
invested in the phone when I'd begun driving again in the
middle of November and had been frightened of being out
in the car alone. During the afternoon, the programme-
makers had to break off to take me for my appointment at
occupational therapy, and when they brought me home that
evening, after eight hours' filming, they wanted to come
with me to the aerobics Christmas party. I actually
managed to say no to them. I needed space, so I sent them
away, switched my mobile off, and got ready to go out and
enjoy myself.

The year before, I'd enjoyed every minute of the aerobics

Christmas party, and had joined in all the fun. But this year I just sat down, wondering why on earth I was there. It was the first time I'd stopped since the end of the court case, and suddenly it all hit me. I went into the loo and cried. I didn't sleep at all that night, but lay crying in the dark.

The next few days were full of more of the same. It was the first time I'd dealt with the phone calls myself – straight after the attack my family had fielded them for me – but now I was fit enough to take them. I didn't find it that stressful to deal with all the people who wanted to speak to me – I'd started to take it all in my stride – and I rushed from one interview to another, my mobile still ringing, and coming home to more messages. Friends suggested I get an agent, but I thought I'd be all right. They said I could be making money out of all this. I had been given occasional payments – one national newspaper gave me £500 because, they said, I'd done so much for them and they'd taken up so much of my time. No doubt I could have made lots more if I'd got an agent and become a professional, but I'd made the decision right from the start that money wasn't at issue. I wasn't prepared to get rich on the back of a story that involved the lives of three children.

Two days after the court case ended, I escaped from the phone calls and interviews for an hour to see the children's Christmas play. The welcome they always gave me – 'Miss Potts is here!' – made me forget the horror for a short time and put stress into the background. The present nursery children weren't taking part, so Ahmed wasn't in it, but all the Reception children had parts. Francesca and Reena were snowflakes. Their faces had been cleverly made up with snowflakes on their cheeks, so their scars weren't visible. They looked so happy; and their beautiful faces shone out from the pages of the next day's *Express & Star*, but I cried when I got home.

It felt so good to have that short time away from the media that I decided to get away from it all for more than just one hour. The time had come to take up my *Nursery World* award of three nights at a health farm. After all we'd been through in court, I decided to ask Linda to come with me, and we booked in from Sunday to Wednesday. On the Saturday before that, though, I went to Nottingham for my brother's graduation. I was so pleased to sit back at a ceremony in which the focus was on Lee, not me, and really excited to watch him walking forward to receive the PhD he'd worked so hard for. Now I'd have to start calling my brother 'Dr Potts'!

Early the next morning, Linda and I set off to be pampered for three days. I left my mobile at home, so I could really get away from everything. The health farm was gorgeous and the staff were very good to us. We had massages, facials and saunas and relaxed so much that one night I slept for thirteen hours. We spent a lot of time walking through the peaceful grounds, talking. I told Linda how difficult I was finding it to accept the great changes in my life, but that in January I'd have a fresh start. Not only was I going back to work, but I'd decided that if I was to have a really new beginning, I should leave home and begin a new independent life. It was nearly a year since my friend from Brownies, Jackie, had asked me to share her house. We'd talked about me moving in during the summer holidays, but the attack had put paid to that idea. Now, I thought, it was the ideal time. The court case was over, I'd had four awards and lots of publicity, and at last I would be left alone to create my life. Mum had been upset when I told her, feeling that I wasn't yet well enough. But Linda sounded more positive about the idea, and I told her I was planning to move between Christmas and New Year.

Linda and I went straight from the health farm to the International Convention Centre in Birmingham for the *Sunday Mercury* Wonderkids awards. Francesca, Reena and Ahmed were running around happily, truly little children of courage. They had the will to fight, and it was so exciting to see them being recognised for it. I was invited to go up and present the award – it was such a pleasure to be giving an award to them, rather than have someone else giving one to me. But talking to Francesca's mum afterwards, I heard how she was suffering emotionally. It was a side of Francesca other people didn't often see; she was another one hiding behind her smile.

From the time the court case ended, there had been a campaign for me to get the George Cross. The *Daily Mail* launched the campaign on 11 December with a front-page headline 'Give them the George Cross'. Underneath the words were pictures of me, Gwen Mayor, the teacher who was killed at Dunblane, and Philip Lawrence, the head teacher who was stabbed to death as he tried to defend a pupil from a gang attack. Inside the paper was a coupon which readers were invited to fill in and return, headed: 'To the Prime Minister, We urge you to recommend Philip Lawrence, Gwen Mayor and Lisa Potts for the George Cross in recognition of their outstanding bravery.' A compilation of quotes in a long article included one from the Bishop of Wolverhampton: 'Lisa went back not once but twice to protect the children. None of us knows how we would react in such a situation but Lisa was wonderful.'

The campaign was a complete shock. It was Denise who asked me if I'd seen the papers, when she picked me up to take me to school for the children's Christmas play, and my first reaction when I read the *Mail* story was embarrassment. How could I collect a medal, when Gwen Mayor and Philip Lawrence had died? I was even more embarrassed when I walked into the staff-room and people started to say, 'You deserve it'. Did I? I wasn't at all sure about that. The campaign was taken up by the *Express & Star*. The editor published a letter he had written to John Major, which began: 'I am writing on behalf of this newspaper, our readers and the town of Wolverhampton to urge the award of the George Cross to nursery nurse Lisa Potts.' His letter was followed by letters to the Prime Minister from our local MP, councillors and police chiefs.

My attention was diverted from the *Mail* story that day, however, by another in the *Express*. Under the headline 'Machete maniac cost me my love', it was reported that the attack had led directly to the break-up of my relationship with Marc, and went on to give details. When the *Express & Star* contacted me later to ask how I felt about the national newspaper speculation, I told them, 'This has really upset me and hurt me. Marc is my best friend and he's been very supportive since the machete attack.' The report upset Marc a great deal too. He felt it was an intrusion into his life, but we talked about it, and still remained good friends afterwards.

I began to receive bagfuls of mail again. All my letters were positive – except one. It read: 'Dear Lisa, You do not deserve the George Cross. I'm appalled that you think you do. Why didn't you save any of your own race that day?' Dad calmly said it was a letter from a racist and should be put in the bin, but I was horrified and frightened to think that anyone would stop to think about the colour of a child's skin before deciding whether or not to save them. And the letter was wrong to say that I thought I deserved the George Cross – I never thought I did.

Letters were pouring into the newspaper office too. The *Express & Star* reported that ninety-eight per cent of their readers supported the campaign, and printed samples of some of their letters. 'All eighteen members of our family have been touched by her bravery and her lovely personality on TV,' one lady wrote. 'She handled every interview with great dignity. Her caring and compassion brought tears to our eyes and those of lots of other people we have spoken to.' Another wrote: 'Lisa's parents must be very proud to have a daughter who put her own life on the line,' and another suggested that, as well as the George Cross, I should get a few thousand from the National Lottery too, adding, 'If I could win it I would give her half myself. She's smashing.' They were such heart-warming comments, and I didn't mind at all the couple of published letters which read: 'She only did (as she says) what anyone would have done,' and: 'In my opinion the degree of courage shown by Lisa Potts, although exceptional, does not meet the criteria for the award of the George Cross. However, the George Medal would be appropriate in the circumstances.' As it turned out, the Queen and Prime Minister must have agreed with him.

A few days later the *Express & Star* reported that a Wolverhampton newsagent had faxed a letter to the Prime Minister offering to fund the cost of the George Cross. 'There is nothing we can give that girl which is big enough to mark what she has done,' he wrote. The matter was even raised at Prime Minister's Question Time in the House of Commons, when Peter Viggers, MP for Gosport, asked John Major to respond to the recent 'extraordinary cases of gallantry'. Mr Major said he couldn't comment, but was sure that what Mr Viggers had said would have been heard 'in the appropriate places'.

I was amazed and touched by all this, and even more so when I read what Jock Gallagher, the press officer at New Cross Hospital, had told the *Express & Star*. He said I had been 'totally and utterly unconcerned' with my own

152

The Midland Diamond Award, October 1996,
presented by some of the nursery children

Christmas 1996 at the Wonderkids Award with
Francesca, Reena and Ahmed

The day I returned to work, January 1997

Me and friends dancing in a show at the Grand Theatre in
Wolverhampton, eight months after the attack

The Daily Star Award, presented by Cherie Blair
at the Savoy Hotel, March 1997

At the Sunshine Awards, sponsored by *The Sun* newspaper,
with Sharon Davies and Anthea Turner

With Tony and Cherie Blair when they visited
St Luke's School, May 1997

The first anniversary of the attack with Maariyah Pathan,
Nakita Banger and Taishion Wynter at Alton Towers

My last day at St Luke's, July 1997

Outside Buckingham Palace with Princess Diana's butler,
Paul Burrell, having received the George Medal,
13 November 1997

My family outside Buckingham Palace

injuries when I arrived at the hospital. 'All she wanted to know was how the children were. It was at that point that I knew we were talking to somebody really special. I felt I was in the company of someone who was genuinely good. I've been a journalist for forty years, but it was the first time I used the phrase heroine and did not think it was an exaggeration.'

People began to stop me in the street saying, 'I hope you get the George Cross,' or, 'I'm sure you'll be in the New Year's Honours List.' I always said something like, 'Whatever will be, will be.' Everywhere I went I could hear my name being whispered, 'That's Lisa Potts.' 'Isn't that Lisa?' 'Look, it's Lisa Potts.' It was a funny feeling to keep on hearing my name as an almost continuous background noise, and it made me nervous. One day I was getting off a packed train when a young teenage girl passed me a short note. 'Dear Lisa, You don't know me, but I would just like to take this opportunity to express how much I admire your bravery and work. I didn't want to approach you on the platform because you must be fed up of people like me. My brother was on his work experience at New Cross at the time and told me how devastating it all was and how courageous you were.' The same thing happened again on another train, this time with a black man, who hadn't wanted to approach me in case I was afraid. And when I arrived at school, Pam Shee would greet me with, 'Lisa, your letters.' Some were addressed to 'Lisa the Brave', 'Lisa the Machete Heroine', or even 'Lisa who is about to get the George Cross'. They had no address, never mind a postcode, but they would reach me at 'Wolverhampton'. I loved replying to the letters, and wrote replies to as many as I could, but it hurt my hand so much and cost a fortune in stamps. The lady at the post office asked if I was setting up a business when I kept arriving with batches of envelopes. My friends were joking with me about the coverage I was getting, laughing at the fact that they knew this great heroine. I honestly didn't think I'd get the George Cross, and I actually dismissed it from my mind, even though letters continued to flood my home, the school and the newspaper offices.

It didn't feel like Christmas. I had lovely presents, but the usual TV programmes and celebrations meant nothing. I was so sad and lost on Christmas Day. It was as if Christmas and the preceding six months all ran together. Discovering I had come second to John Major as the Radio Four *Today Programme* Personality of the Year, and second to Princess Diana in the Teletext Woman of the Year, made me feel all the more mixed up. Lisa Potts alongside a Princess and the Prime Minister. What on earth was going on?

My feelings were so confused, with the attack, the awards, the court case, people stopping me in the street, the media attention and the campaign for the George Cross. Again, I was wondering who I was – an ordinary nursery nurse or a heroine and celebrity? I didn't seem to fit into either category. Not knowing who I was any more, I wasn't ready for the emotions involved in forming a new relationship. So when a new man came into my life, it was hard for me to cope with being part of a couple again. We got on really well and he was so funny, which is what I needed at that point. He had an amazing ability to make me laugh, even when I was feeling very down. I started to become close to him, but I knew there were times when I hurt him because I was so mixed up inside. I didn't seem to have much control over my emotions, and as a result I sometimes treated him badly. I was still thinking a lot about Marc, because I'd been with him for such a long time. I didn't seem to have much time, either, for getting to know this man properly. I hadn't found myself again, and it was difficult for him because he didn't know the Lisa before the attack. He was learning about me at the same time as I was learning about myself. Our relationship couldn't last in these circumstances. It continued on and off for a few months, and each time it went wrong I tried to make it better, but it never worked. I realised it had no future until I had given myself more time alone. I felt so guilty that not only was it all over with Marc, but this new relationship hadn't worked out either. My psychologist told me it was all part of what I was going through, and I realise now that it wasn't all my fault, so I couldn't blame myself.

I was looking forward to my fresh start in January, although Mum was upset that I was moving out. I kept telling her it was only a ten-minute drive up the road, and I really did think it was the best thing for me to do. On 29 December, Dad, Marc and Clare's dad helped me move all my possessions, clothes and furniture to Jackie's house. I had been due to be interviewed by *Hello* magazine on 30 December, but I phoned to cancel. It was supposed to be an 'At Home' feature with me and my parents, and I had to explain that the day before I was meant to be 'at home', I was moving out. My friends laughed at me, saying I must really have gone up in the world if I could cancel a magazine like *Hello*.

There was only a week to go before I returned to St Luke's, so I set about creating my new room, expecting to enjoy every minute. But almost immediately, I started to miss home so much. I got on really well with Jackie, but it wasn't a busy household like ours, and life wasn't the same without my parents. I missed Clare being across the road too. I was allergic to Jackie's cat, which hadn't bothered me too much before, but living there all the time meant I got a permanent rash and sore throat. After a few days I told Jackie I'd have to move out. She laughed – it had taken so long to move my things and sort them out, and now I was leaving. I never told Mum how much I'd missed her – I just blamed the cat for my decision to go back home. It snowed on the weekend of 4–5 January, when I enlisted help to move all my things back home again. We were still moving the wardrobe at eleven o'clock on the Sunday night, even though I was due to go back to work the following morning, for the first time in six months.

I'd had a meeting with the education department about the return to school, and Denise had checked with me to make sure I really was all right to go back. Friends and family were telling me it was too early to return, but I felt I had to go back, to face up to my fears. In the event I didn't have any time to worry about how I'd feel about it. I slept that night surrounded by boxes, having only had time to unpack the clothes I wanted to wear on my first day back. Being interviewed live at 6.30 the next morning on GMTV was hilarious. I felt like telling them that I'd moved house twice in the last week and I'd spent the night with all my possessions piled up around me. Radio stations were phoning constantly, making me ten minutes late for my first day back. I eventually went off to school in the snow, to face more press waiting for me as I pulled up at the school gates. 'Why?' I wondered. After all, I was only going back to work. The morning was full of interviews and press photographs with the children, and I was back on live TV for the lunchtime news. The first day was a media circus. My first proper day back with the children wasn't until the next day.

I was glad to be back, and wanted the interviews out of the way so I could get on with my work. I didn't know then that this was the start of the worst six months of my life – much worse, emotionally, than the six months I'd just been through. I had genuinely thought that with the court case being over, the media attention would stop and I could slip back into being a normal nursery nurse. I even thought that being back at school would help me to lead a normal life again. But the fresh start wasn't to be. My house move had lasted all of five days, and now the ordeal of school was to prove so much worse than I could possibly have anticipated. I'd wanted to return to school to lay the ghosts; I didn't want to think it was impossible for me to go back. The children had gone back, so why shouldn't I? I didn't want them to think of me as the nursery nurse who couldn't go back to school. But the horror to come took me by surprise.

A post had been created for me at the school; there was a new nursery nurse in the nursery. At first I'd felt sad not to be working in there, but I realised when I visited the nursery on my second day back that it was much better that I wasn't. It didn't feel like the place I'd known and, except for Ahmed, I knew hardly any of the children in there. I also felt that Dorothy Hawes was having some difficulties in relating to me, which I suppose was understandable. My new post involved 'floating' between the two Reception classes, and I was happy to be working with the children who had been in the nursery the previous year. I couldn't give myself totally to one class as the 'fixed' nursery nurse, because I still had to go so often to my occupational therapy or psychologist appointments. The children were fascinated each time I came back from occupational therapy with different splints on my arm. Once I had silicon put on my arm to flatten the scar, which they thought was very impressive. They were very helpful, understanding that there were things I couldn't do because of my injuries, and helped me by holding pictures down while I was putting glue on the back, or cutting bits of sticky tape for me. But I felt less and less like Miss Potts the nursery nurse, especially when some of the children called me 'Lisa', because that's how I was known in the media. I had become someone on TV, not their old nursery nurse. I somehow felt I didn't fit in at the school any more, even though everyone was supportive and understood that I had to keep leaving school for various visits.

These visits weren't only to the hospital. I also had time off over the next few months because I'd become the school's unofficial representative. So many people raised money for St Luke's, including the local pub, the Rose and Crown. There were many local factories and businesses which had cheques to present, and I went to collect the cheques on behalf of the school. On one occasion I was invited to London by Rothschild Banking to give a talk about what had happened and to be presented with another cheque. I also spoke at charity functions and opened nurseries. When I received a cheque from the factory where Marc worked, I found the employees had dipped into their pockets to raise £125 as a gift for me to get myself something.

The school had changed by the time I returned. There was no longer a three-foot fence round the nursery: a new six-foot fence stood in its place. Every teacher had been given a panic alarm the term before, and it became a standing joke that I was the only one who didn't have one. There was now only one entrance into the school building, and this had digital locking. Some parents wanted even more done in the way of security, and I could understand both points of view; there shouldn't be the easy access that we'd had before, but neither should the school become a prison.

Although work wasn't too bad for the first few days, I had lost the joy of it. I was happy to be with the children, but I no longer loved to get up in the morning as I had before. And within a week the real difficulties began. I started to have severe flashbacks, sometimes fifteen times during the school day. If a child screamed when I was in the playground with them, I'd panic. When a child tapped me on the back to get my attention, I saw Horrett Campbell hitting me on the back. If I looked out of the window and saw someone I didn't know walking past, I imagined he was going to jump the fence. Sometimes I'd just stand at the window and stare at the nursery playground, seeing the whole attack happening before my eyes. The very smell of the school brought the attack to my mind. I couldn't get to sleep at night for hours, and when I did, my nightmares were terrible. I had a maximum of four hours sleep every night, and each day it was harder to get up. I became terribly tired, and I didn't enjoy life at all, even having to give up aerobics because of my exhaustion. The pain in my arm was dreadful, and was particularly bad when I was in school because of the physical movement involved in fastening buttons and tying laces.

After a few weeks a day came when things were so bad that I had to tell someone about it. I'd had a terrible night, waking hot and sweating from one nightmare after another. In one awful dream I'd been trapped in the nursery, forced to watch Ahmed being struck again and again on his head. His face was pressed against the window and he was staring at me, but I was stuck inside and there was nothing I could do to help him. In another nightmare, which recurred for months, I was lying in bed, all dressed in white, when Horrett Campbell approached me carrying a huge knife. He stabbed me straight through my body, and the knife went through the bed and through the floor to the room below. I got up and ran downstairs to get a bucket to put underneath the knife and catch the blood which was pouring from it, then put the bucket in the fridge so it would keep my blood fresh. After a night like that, I had to drag myself to school, and I felt so exhausted that I fell asleep at lunchtime. I lost count of the flashbacks I suffered that day. One of the children offered me a teddy bear crisp like the ones we'd had at the picnic, and just the smell of them took me straight back to the horror of the attack.

I'd kept my difficulties to myself until then, but that evening when I went out with Nici I cried and cried. I told her I couldn't go on at work any more. I decided I should tell Mum, too, and she said I didn't have to go back if I didn't want to. She said she wouldn't even have gone back in the first place. But I pulled myself together and said I felt the children needed me to stay at least until they moved up to their next class. Yet in the next breath I was saying I was no good to them; I might just be a reminder of the attack. I felt so worried about them. In fact, I spent a lot of time worrying, which wasn't like me. Eventually I made up my mind to stay until May half-term, and if I was no better then, I'd resign. That meant another three months, but at least I had a deadline to work towards.

I was still doing interviews regularly with various magazines and papers, and wondered if I should admit to the flashbacks and nightmares. But I decided not to, yet. I still put on my smile for the public – it was what they expected of me, after all. I was still 'brave Lisa Potts' to them, and now it was more than six months since the attack, people thought I'd be 'over it'. They had no idea that I was crushed because I was longing to be a normal nursery nurse at school, yet school was the very place that was wearing me down. I'd thought I would be better when I got back to school; that a new life would begin. But everything was so much worse than before, not better. Yet what else could I do?

Those months weren't all full of horror; there were a few good times too. I went to camp with some Year Two children and really enjoyed it. I also kept going to Brownies, and realised that I was better when I was out of the school setting. I had a letter from Hodder & Stoughton, asking me to meet them to discuss me writing a children's prayer book. I felt so positive about it. It was a lovely idea to work on a book which would include the children's prayers as well as my own and, because it was something I was doing for myself, it would give me a great sense of achievement. One thing I didn't give up was rehearsals for the dancing show, which was coming up in March. I felt very nervous about the show; my arm was still so painful, and the other girls had to spend hours giving me extra tuition to make up for the months I'd missed. But I was determined to be in every dance: it would be another achievement. The old Lisa was doing this – not the new Lisa who collected awards for bravery or cheques for St Luke's.

I was relieved when it was February half-term. When I wasn't doing interviews or going to meetings with the union to sort out my compensation, I spent the time working on the prayer book. It really helped to take my mind off school. Writing the introduction to the prayer book was great therapy, so I decided to continue writing down how I was feeling. After half-term I began to develop a calmness while I was at work. It was a conscious choice; I could choose to remain calm, or I could choose not to. And if I was going to stay for at least another three months, there wasn't really any choice. I never had an evening where I got home from school, had dinner and watched TV. I was busier than ever with presentations and interviews, and with many of them taking place after school or in the evenings, it made me even more tired. I began making recordings for the BBC's *First Light* programme after school. One evening I was invited to a special school in Hereford to open a further education department, and the following day a photographer came to the house after school to take shots of me for an exhibition he was doing on women of the nineties. Nearly everything I did came out of the attack, because I'd now been made some kind of celebrity. I could have said no, but I didn't know how. When the assignments took place in school time, I was guilty to realise that I felt relieved to be away from St Luke's. I was invited to London's Broadcasting House in schooltime to accept a cheque for being runner-up on Personality of the Year. The cheque for over £1000, which was for St Luke's, represented the money generated by my telephone votes.

At the end of February I had a phone call from Gerry Watson at Bass Brewery to tell me I'd been nominated as Midlander of the Year. I was invited to a big dinner and presentation in May. I asked how many others had been nominated, and he said, 'No, Lisa, you *are* the Midlander of the Year.' He told me I'd been selected by a panel which included representatives from all sections of the media and was chaired by the Lord Lieutenant for the County of West Midlands. I was speechless, for once. The annual award was aimed at 'the person considered to have increased the prestige of the region or [who] has made an outstanding contribution to the social, political, industrial or cultural life of the area'. I had won, he said, not only because of my bravery, but because of my commitment to children through my continued work with Brownies, holiday clubs, crèche and special contribution to Children in Need. He made an appointment to come into school the following week to take photographs of me with the children. When he arrived, he brought a massive cake with the words 'Lisa

Potts, St Luke's, Midlander of the Year'. We took it into the hall and put it on the floor while the children and I prepared for the photographs. The mother and toddler group was meeting in there, and one little child gave his opinion of the proceedings by tottering over and putting his hand right on the cake. We managed to patch it up so it looked all right when the pictures were taken. I told the assembled press I still couldn't believe I was to receive such a prestigious award, but I was proud to receive it on behalf of St Luke's and the children.

My birthday was very different from my happy twenty-first of the year before. I was grateful that everyone made such an effort to give me a good time, but I didn't feel like celebrating. This birthday was spent like nearly every day – in pain, having flashbacks, feeling exhausted and worrying about school. Three days after my birthday, Horrett Campbell was sentenced at Teeside Crown Court. Mr Justice Sedley said Campbell should be detained indefinitely at a secure mental hospital under Section thirty-seven of the Mental Health Act. The judge said it was 'a relief to know Campbell was seriously ill', because to believe such an act could be done by a sane person would shake his belief in humanity. He also criticised the authorities for the delay in 'rewarding Lisa's bravery'. I was working at St Luke's when Carol phoned to tell me the sentence. I felt relieved that another chapter had ended, but still I had the local paper coming to the school to interview me on my reaction to the sentence.

11 Deciding to Leave St Luke's

A couple of weeks later I took another step on my road to recovery with the day of the dancing show. I felt so happy and excited as we sorted out our dressing-rooms and costumes, rehearsed and went out to lunch together. Just before the show, however, I began to think, 'What if there's someone out there who pulls out a gun and shoots me?' Any one of the hundreds of people in the theatre could run onto the stage and stab me, or shoot me from where they were sitting. As we went on for our very first dance, I was terrified. The curtains went up, and all I could see was bright light. People could see me, but I couldn't see them. All through the dance I was frightened, and only occasionally did I think about what I was meant to be doing. But as soon as the dance finished, the audience clapped as if they'd never stop, and behind the scenes all the girls hugged me and said I'd done so well. After that I was fine; I stopped thinking about being attacked and started to enjoy the dances. When the whole show was over I felt wonderful. I had a great sense of achievement and I wanted to do it all over again, even though my arm was unbearably painful. I felt such gratitude towards my dancing teacher and all the girls who supported me. I had been so worried that I'd mess it up for everyone.

There was more excitement to come the following week. Lee and I travelled down to London, where I was to receive my Gold Star bravery award from the *Daily Star* newspaper. All the winners had been told there was another surprise for them the day before the awards, so we travelled down early. As we gathered in the hotel, waiting for the coach to take us to the mystery destination, I met my thirteen fellow award-winners. They included Roger de Graaf, who saved hundreds of people in the IRA Docklands blast, and Chris Moon, who completed the London Marathon only months after losing his leg and hand when clearing landmines in Mozambique. There were also children to be honoured – a ten-year-old who saved a student from drowning, and a nine-year-old who rescued twenty horses in a riding school fire.

We all piled into the coach and had a tour round London, ending up at Downing Street. We were amazed when the coach stopped and we were asked to get out – to be led inside for tea at Number Ten with John and Norma Major. I had to pinch myself when John Major came over to talk to me. Was this real? He asked how I was and told me I'd been extremely brave. Someone called over, 'Do you know if she's going to get the George Cross?' I wanted the ground to open and swallow me up, but he just smiled and carried on talking to me. I found myself telling him that when I got married I'd wear a wedding dress that covered my scars, and immediately I asked myself, 'Why did I say that to the Prime Minister of the country?' But I was just being my usual self, I didn't feel any need to put on an act. Norma Major chatted to me for quite a long time while arrangements were made for a group photograph.

A little later, a man came up to talk to me. His badge said, 'Mr Mayor, City of Dunblane'. I thought he was the Mayor of Dunblane, and I started talking to him about the massacre there. Eventually he told me his wife was Gwen Mayor, the teacher who had been killed. I was so shocked, and tears began to drip down my face. I didn't know what to say to him – how could I have not realised who he was when I'd read his badge? He was there to receive an award on behalf of Dunblane. We started talking about the weapons, and agreed that if Campbell had had a gun, like Thomas Hamilton, there would have been many deaths at St Luke's too. I admired him so much, but I felt terribly guilty afterwards. His wife had been killed, and I hadn't. I couldn't sleep that night for thinking about it.

When we got back to the hotel Lee didn't believe me when I told him where we'd been. He kept saying 'Never!' and laughing. At dinner that night we sat with Tony Bullimore, the yachtsman who had survived five days in the hull of his upturned yacht, and his wife Lal. They were great company and I loved listening to the fantastic stories they had to tell. And the following day, at the award ceremony, I met so many more amazing people. There were sports personalities, stars from TV soaps, singers and models. But again I thought, 'They're just ordinary people, I don't need to get my autograph book out.' There were more press outside the Savoy than I'd ever seen at one of these ceremonies – but that was because Princess Diana was going to be there.

Inside the hotel, Cherie Blair came up and hugged me. She clearly knew so much about my story – the court case, the awards and my return to work. She chatted to Lee too, and was so down-to-earth and friendly. When we had all found our seats in the ballroom, we were asked to stand for Diana, Princess of Wales. As she walked in, she passed so close to me, and sat at the next table. It was so hard to believe that I was sitting so near to the Princess, Cherie Blair and Norma Major, and at the same table as Jeremy

Beadle, Chris Tarrant and lots of other famous people. I should have been at work.

After the dinner came the award presentation, and I cried for them all. Rodney Mayor received the Dunblane award just before me, and I was in floods of tears. I don't know how I recovered my composure enough to walk to the front, especially when I'd also had to listen to the editor of the *Daily Star*, in his commendation, say that the children of St Luke's would remember me as 'the brave, beautiful shining face of a guardian angel who saved their lives'. I was so overwhelmed as I concentrated on walking forward, telling myself to hold my back straight and not fall over. I passed Richard Branson, who smiled at me. When Cherie Blair put the ribbon over my head, everyone stood up and the thunderous applause went on and on. It didn't stop until I got back to my seat. As I walked past Princess Diana she winked at me and mouthed the words 'Well done.'

I sat there for the rest of the ceremony feeling guilty. Hundreds of people had stood up for me, but what about the rest of the people who were receiving awards? I wasn't any more brave than them. Princess Diana gave Chris Moon his award – why weren't we standing for him? I knew that Mum and Dad would be so excited to see the award and hear all about it when I got home, but I also knew that to me it was just another one to put on the mantelpiece with the rest. I already knew I had three more big award ceremonies coming up in the next weeks. It wasn't that the awards weren't special, or that I didn't feel honoured to receive them, but I never forgot that they came out of a couple of minutes of horror, when I'd done something that I believe anyone would have done in those circumstances.

Life went from one extreme to the other, because after all the excitement of the ceremony I was back to school the next day, battling against fear. Caring for thirty children at school, while not sleeping and having terrible flashbacks and nightmares, was taking its toll. I knew I was making progress with the children, but every day I looked at Francesca and thought again that if my hand had been only slightly higher, she wouldn't have that scar. I was so glad that the following week the school was breaking up for the Easter holidays. And during the holidays two things happened that would aid my recovery.

The first was very simple. I knew I had to do something different to get rid of the tension and frustration I was feeling, so I suggested to Nicola that we should join a gym. We found one a few miles out of Wolverhampton, where I wouldn't be recognised so readily, and we began to go there twice a week. I firmly believe that exercise is the best way to get rid of tension, and I started to benefit from it straight away, even though I had many difficulties with my arm. I realised too that I needed more help than I was having. The psychologist appointments were good in their own way, but it wasn't enough. I had also been meeting Shirley, one of the leaders on the church young people's weekend, at her house. With the vicar from her church, we had met weekly to talk about school and about my faith, and it had been helpful. Even so, I felt so torn apart with my emotions and I knew I was starting to take my feelings out on those closest to me. Friends had suggested counselling, which sounded a good idea.

During the Easter holidays I found the answer. The father of one of my Brownies was a counsellor for Acorns, a children's hospice in Birmingham. He invited me to visit the hospice, which was a fantastic, yet heartbreaking, experience. Many charities had written to ask me to support them in various ways, and I hadn't known how to choose. Once I'd seen Acorns I knew I could commit myself to helping them. I decided immediately to give part of the royalties from my prayer book to Acorns, and if I was occasionally offered money for public appearances I would ask them to write a cheque to the hospice. On the way home in the car, Phil asked me what type of counselling I'd been having. I decided to tell him how I was feeling, and he could tell I needed more help. He said he'd like to come round and meet Mum, and if we agreed, he would become my counsellor. He said he wanted to do something for me, because I'd looked after his daughter on Brownie pack holiday when she'd been ill. The following week he came to our house and met Mum, then talked with me for an hour. We went through things slowly and in detail. He sat and listened, never suggesting what I should or shouldn't do. It was so helpful, and we agreed to meet fortnightly after that.

The Easter holiday was hectic with magazine interviews and with filming the *Headliners* programme for Central TV, but the fact that I'd joined the gym and started counselling made me feel more positive. So when term started again it was a shock. I felt even worse than I had the term before. One night I only slept from midnight to one o'clock, then lay awake in the dark. I was exhausted, and decided I must talk to Denise about it. She was very understanding, and suggested I take time off as sick leave. It was tempting, but I didn't want to give in. I decided I could fight it.

Part of the reason I wanted to carry on was because I didn't want to miss Tony and Cherie Blair's visit to St Luke's. They were coming to Wolverhampton as part of the election campaign, and Cherie had sent me a hand-written note to say how much she was looking forward to seeing me again. When they arrived she came straight to me to ask how I was. I sat with Tony Blair while he ate beans and pizza for his school dinner, and the press took photos of us. They chatted to the children about everyday things, and Cherie told her husband to stand in the queue with his tray to scrape away any leftovers when he'd finished. It was all so natural. In the playground one of the children said to Cherie, 'Miss, can I look at your ring?' and she took it off and tried it on all the children's fingers. One called to Tony Blair, 'Are you friends with John Major?' and he laughed.

The next day Mum, Dad, Pam and I travelled with Francesca, Reena, Ahmed and their parents to London to receive the Sunshine Award from *The Sun* newspaper. Before the award ceremony the children and I were invited onto the *This Morning* show with Richard and Judy. We had to go by car and Ahmed was sick, so when we arrived at the TV studios he had to be given a *This Morning* T-shirt to wear. In front of the cameras, the children didn't say a word, so I did all the talking – as usual! Josie Russell was there with her father. She was receiving a Sunshine award too. The attack in which her mother and sister had been killed had happened the day after the St Luke's attack. We were rushed back to the Kensington Roof Gardens for the award ceremony, where the media were waiting for us. Mum and Dad were already there, chatting to Terry Wogan and Anthea Turner, who were presenting the awards. When she saw me, Anthea Turner said she felt she knew me already, having interviewed me so often by satellite on GMTV.

There were so many people there from the pop world, including Boyzone and East 17. Louise from Eternal came over and hugged me and, pictured with me in *The Sun* the next day, she was quoted as saying, 'I am in total admiration of you.' They also quoted Tessa Sanderson, who said she had felt 'truly humbled' by shaking hands with me. One of the boys from East 17 said to me, 'I hope you get the main award today.' I had no idea there was a main award, although if I'd read the newspaper I would have known. The newspaper's readers had voted for the award-winners and, as I was amazed to discover later, I'd received the most votes, and Josie Russell was the runner-up.

Francesca, Reena and Ahmed received their awards before me, and were given a trip to Eurodisney. I was so glad for them, and so proud as they walked forward. Nearly everyone was in tears. When it was my turn, I was given a cheque for £5000 from *The Sun* and a two-week holiday for two in America from Virgin holidays. Mum and Dad were so pleased that I'd been given something for myself. I was thrilled with the money. I could put it towards a car with power steering, which would make driving so much easier for me. It seemed a huge amount to me, earning only £9000 a year as I was. But the next day when I went to buy a copy of *The Sun*, on the front cover of which the children and I appeared, the lady in the newsagent's said, 'I bet you're absolutely stinking rich now – £5000, plus all the money you've earned this year.' I told her I hadn't been earning anything much, except for my salary. 'Haven't you, darlin'? Didn't you sign one of them exclusives and get thousands?' she said. I explained why I'd decided not to do that, but she found it difficult to believe. Like many people, she thought that if I wasn't earning anything from all the magazine and newspaper interviews, and the TV and radio appearances, why was I doing it? If I told people it was because I couldn't say no, they just laughed at me. Another person said, 'I bet you're glad the attack happened – all this high life you're living now.' I laughed it off, but it hurt all the same.

Two weeks after Denise had suggested I take sick leave, I decided to go along with the suggestion. I was mentally and physically drained. The night I left school, Friday 18 April, I went to stay with Dawn. I cried and talked all night. I asked her if I was right to take time off, when I'd already been off work for six months. She said it was the best thing. And she was right. Mum had suggested I had a holiday, to get away not just from school but from everything. So Donna, a friend from Brownies and crèche, came with me to Gran Canaria. On that holiday I had no flashbacks, no nightmares, and slept at least eight hours a night. It was the most fantastic week, sunbathing, reading and relaxing.

We met two lads and a girl who were staying in the hotel, and became friendly. After a few days, when the girl was rubbing sun cream into my back, she asked me how I'd got my scars. It was so refreshing to be asked by someone who genuinely didn't know. I told her and, of course, she then realised who I was. She told her friends, and one of them, Paul, told me about an experience he'd had when he was working at his university's student union. He saw a man attacking a woman, and when he ran over to defend her, he was stabbed through the heart. He had spent six months in rehabilitation, and for a long time lost the feeling down one side of his body. He'd suffered terrible flashbacks and nightmares. At last I had met someone who identified with me and who could tell me that things do get easier, that you do lose the desire to talk about it all the time. I learnt so much, and I knew that life could get better. I felt as if I'd been sent there to meet him. Donna and I spent the rest of the week with them, and we have remained in contact since. I knew when I got home I could phone Paul and he would easily relate to whatever I was going through.

At the end of the holiday I felt so much stronger. I was totally relaxed, and the thought of going back to school was terrifying. I didn't want to be lazy, but I felt I needed more time off, so the doctor gave me another certificate. I still went into school a couple of times a week to see the children, and once or twice I worked a full day. I couldn't have coped with school as well as all the things I was doing in May. I flew to Glasgow where I stayed two nights, to present some films for the *Fully Booked* children's programme. As a result of that the producer asked me to do some interviewing and presenting at Birmingham Repertory Theatre the next week with the Rambert Ballet. This was something I enjoyed doing; in its own way it was as relaxing as being on holiday. I enjoyed working on TV, especially when it wasn't about the attack.

The next day I had to cram in the occupational therapist, psychologist, counsellor, doctor and hairdresser, none of whom I'd had time to see for two weeks, before the Midlander of the Year award ceremony the day after. I was allowed to invite nine people to the ceremony, and had hoped one of them could be Dawn, but as her baby was due on the same day it didn't seem safe. Mum, Dad and Pam came, as well as Lee and his girlfriend Helen. Then I asked three people from St Luke's, Denise, Kath and Pam Shee, and my friend Nici. We were taken by limousine to Birmingham where the most fantastic evening awaited us, all filmed by Central TV for the *Headliners* programme. I sat at the top table, and in front of me in huge shiny writing were the words 'Lisa Potts, Midlander of the Year'. For the first time at one of these occasions, the whole evening revolved around me. It was embarrassing, but I suppose I wasn't too nervous because by then I was used to people staring at me, and I was relaxed because I wasn't at work and was sleeping better.

After the dinner, there were tributes from the Chief Constable of West Mercia and the Provost of Birmingham.

Sue Beardsmore gave a speech and presented the award, and then it was time for me to make my first speech – there would be many more in the future. I hadn't made notes, so I rambled on about how wonderful it was to be there. I found myself chatting to them about all sorts of things, such as how the paramedic had cut my Next cardigan in the ambulance. I don't know if I made much sense, but they all stood to clap me afterwards, and I discovered I'd enjoyed speaking publicly. It was another skill I'd found.

At the back of my mind all the way through was Dawn – had she gone into labour yet? As soon as we got home I phoned her, and was relieved to find I hadn't missed anything. Dawn still hadn't given birth five days later, when I went to another ceremony, this time the Gloucestershire Macmillan Cancer Relief Woman of the Year. I asked Louise to this occasion – I wanted to include everyone, so tried to invite different people to each ceremony. Once again, it meant another new outfit. Because my photograph was taken every time, I felt I had to wear something different. My friends made fun of me, but I wasn't buying expensive gowns. I just did the best I could with the money I had. I was given a certificate and silver bracelet by Lady Appersley, and yet again I had a standing ovation. Lady Appersley was presented with a bouquet with sunflowers in it, and when I told her they were my favourite flowers, she gave me the bouquet, saying, 'You deserve it more than me.'

At home again, I rang again to check on Dawn, but there was no sign of the baby arriving. The next day I went over to take Ashley to school, something I'd done every morning since Dawn had passed her due date. Soon after I arrived home the phone rang: Dawn was having contractions. She didn't want to ring Terry and bring him home from work, as she'd done that twice already and both had been false alarms, so she asked me to take her to hospital. It was very interesting to find that I started to panic and rush round the house, while Dawn, when I collected her, was perfectly calm. I expect I wasn't calm because this was happening to somebody else, not to me. It could also have had something to do with the fact that Anne Diamond and a Central TV film crew were due at my house at one o'clock, and I suspected I wouldn't be ready for them.

As soon as we arrived at New Cross Hospital, Dawn's waters broke and we went straight into the delivery room. I phoned Terry at work, and told Dawn that as soon as he arrived, I'd go. She begged me to stay, grabbing my hand during each contraction, which was agony for me. Dawn gave birth shortly before half past twelve, and I was there for the whole thing. It was the best day of the whole year. I stood at the foot of the bed watching the miracle of a new life emerging. I wept constantly, and still can't get over what must be the most amazing experience ever. The little boy, Iwan, was given to Dawn first, then to Terry, then to me. I gazed at the tiny new creation, then was brought back to reality when I realised I had twenty-five minutes left to get home to start filming with Anne Diamond. I cried all the way home in the car. At one set of traffic lights a man in the car next to me wound down his window and said, 'Are you all right, Lisa?' I nodded, and he said, 'Are you sure? Do you want to stop and talk about it?' I told this perfect stranger that I was crying because my cousin had just had a baby. I had to pull up outside a chemist on the way to buy some eye drops so my eyes wouldn't be bright red for the camera.

I made it home to find our front room in bright light, all set up like a TV studio. Anne Diamond arrived two minutes after me and I told her all about Dawn and the baby, and we talked about the miracle of birth. I was shell-shocked, thinking this couldn't really be my life – interviews, meeting famous people, awards, and watching people having babies. I managed to pull myself together enough to get through the one-hour interview, then changed and went for a long walk in the fields by myself.

It was the first time I'd ever walked far by myself, but since then I've loved going for walks if I've needed to think. I can get a lot of thought out of a walk. On this first one, I asked myself where my life was going. Was it the right thing for me to leave work altogether? Was I going to be happy away from work, and how much would I miss the children? I was much better away from work – but if I left I'd have no job and no money. But then, what's money? Was God telling me to do something different? Had the attack happened for a reason, and if so, was I missing what it was? I knew I needed much more time to heal; I hadn't given myself time, but had rushed from one thing to another. I wasn't settled in any way, and had proved that I couldn't form new relationships because I was no longer sure who I was. I knew if I did leave work, I mustn't rush into a major decision about what to do next, but would have to give myself a break. God would let me know soon enough what I should do, when the time was right. By the time I came back from that walk I had made my decision. I had to find the new me, and I couldn't do that until I left work.

12 Goodbyes and a New Life

I talked my decision through with my family and friends over the weekend. Nearly everyone thought it was the right thing to do; I would heal properly if I left work. I was glad to have so many people behind me when I went to talk to Denise about it. She was very kind, saying she respected my decision but they would all miss me. She said she would speak to the education authority to see if they could find me a new role, still working with children but away from the classroom. I agreed, and when someone from the education authority contacted me with their ideas, I listened to them. But it was no use. I had to accept that a fresh start meant getting away from education in Wolverhampton altogether. Two weeks after the day of my first long walk, I handed in my notice.

There were only a few weeks of term left, and I went into school as much as I could, by arrangement with Denise. I wanted to be with the children as much as possible, but at the same time I felt happy that I was going to leave. I didn't realise then how much I was going to miss them. As usual, I was still busy with many other things too. With William Roache (Ken Barlow from *Coronation Street*) I helped Lancashire police launch a security video for schools. I filmed a pilot programme for the BBC's

Here and Now with the children, and I was the guest at a high school prizegiving in Evesham. I went down to Brighton for the Unison annual conference, where I was presented with a certificate of merit for bravery. I was being honoured again, and given a standing ovation by the huge audience again, but that day I felt lost inside myself. In my hotel bed that night I experienced the most severe nightmares I'd had. I watched Horrett Campbell killing all the children one by one in the playground. It was all in slow motion, and at the end I was the only one left alive. When I awoke I felt terribly claustrophobic, and at four o'clock in the morning I threw back the sheets, which were dripping with sweat, and got out of the room in a panic. I pulled on my tracksuit and trainers and ran down to Brighton beach, where I sat alone for almost two hours. It calmed me, as I sat staring out to sea, having another quiet thinking session.

Meanwhile, I was keeping a secret. On 31 May a letter had arrived with a Ten Downing Street stamp on the back. I was chatting to Mum on her bed when Dad came running in with it. There was great excitement as I opened it and read that I'd been awarded the George Medal. The news wouldn't come out until 14 June, so I wasn't to tell anyone. Dad rang Lee straight away, and I had to tell him not to ring anyone else. I knew it was going to be difficult for us to keep quiet about it for two weeks, especially for Dad, who had been so keen for me to receive it. It didn't seem real, and only when Mum and Dad had gone out, about two hours later, did I sit down and stare at the letter, thinking, 'I've got the George Medal and I'm going to see the Queen to receive it – me, Lisa Potts.' I tried saying it to myself: 'Lisa Potts GM'. But although I knew it would be such a thrill for all the people who'd campaigned, for myself I knew I was still ordinary Lisa Potts with a medal.

All the same, I was bursting to tell all my friends when I saw them that night – and I did tell one or two, who I knew would keep quiet about it.

On 13 June the phone hardly stopped. All the papers wanted to prepare their stories for the next day, when the embargo was lifted, and I was interviewed and photographed all day long. So of course I knew I was going to be in all the papers the next day, but what I didn't expect was to see myself on the front page of every single one. When I walked into the newsagent on 14 June, everyone had been looking at the papers and they all looked up and stared at me. It would have been funny if it hadn't been so embarrassing, and my first instinct was to run out of the shop. But I had to stop and buy the papers first. All the people in the shop began to congratulate me, and in the street on the way home I was hugged and kissed.

I got home as fast as I could to read the papers. 'Georgeous!' was the headline in *The Mirror*, while the *Daily Mail* had 'Queen's Salute to Lisa the Brave'. *The Times* headline included the news that other people were receiving honours too: 'Honours for courage of school staff – George Medal for Lisa Potts and bravery awards for Philip Lawrence and teachers of Dunblane'. Philip Lawrence had been awarded the Queen's Gallantry Medal, while three teachers shot in Dunblane were awarded the Queen's Commendation for Bravery. One of the papers pointed out that only twenty-three George Medals had been awarded in the last ten years, which made me feel even more honoured. I'd been more open than usual in the interviews I'd given the day before, and several of the papers told of my flashbacks and nightmares, my sick leave from school, and the fact that I would soon leave St Luke's. I'd told *The Sun*, 'I'll never get rid of the nightmares while I work at the school. I will miss the children terribly but I cannot get on with my life while I am reminded daily of what happened.'

Paul, the lad I'd met on holiday, had invited me to his party in Surrey that night. I was glad to drive down there in the afternoon and get away from the press attention – there had been many more interviews that day. It was a strange experience to stop for coffee at the motorway services, though. People who had been reading the papers started bobbing their heads up and down, looking up and staring at me in disbelief, then looking down again at the picture in front of them. A man opposite me said, 'I'm not being rude, but is this you?' I said it certainly was, and he jumped up, saying, 'Let me shake your hand!' Then he announced to everyone, 'This is Lisa Potts, isn't she amazing!' I felt so silly. I just wanted the ground to open and swallow me up. But I had to accept it. What else could I do? I couldn't run to the other side of the world. I did manage to escape from it all at Paul's party that night, and although he opened champagne for me, it was good to be away from my home town and to be treated like anyone else.

It was only three weeks until the first anniversary of the attack, and although I was busy during those weeks, it was constantly at the back of my mind. As well as going into school on some days, and the continuing occupational therapy and magazine interviews (including at last the *Hello* 'At Home' interview I'd put off the previous December), I opened the New Cross Hospital Garden Party and launched a scheme for girls' football in Wolverhampton. I judged the Tumble Tot of the Year competition (although I was the worst person they could possibly have asked, because I couldn't make up my mind!), and went to Cardiff to receive a gold medal in the Provincial Police awards. I was thrilled that Philippa Parlor and Linda were also presented with silver medals. I felt so excited as they went forward for their bravery awards; it was as if I wasn't getting one myself. I also tried to reply to some of the many letters which flooded in again once the news of the George Medal broke, including a lovely handwritten note from Cherie Blair and another from Prince Andrew.

But however busy I was, I couldn't stop 8 July coming round. I started to sleep very badly and my mind was full of what I'd been doing the year before, when we were innocently preparing for the teddy bears' picnic. The night before the anniversary, I cried and cried for the children. All the 'if only' thoughts crowded into my mind, and I had to force myself to stop and to tell myself I had done my best. I had some lovely phone calls from people letting me know they were thinking of me as I prepared to face the next day. At least I didn't have any nightmares that night, but that was only for the simple reason that I didn't get a minute's sleep. I knew the day ahead was going to be one of mixed emotions. A Wolverhampton police charity, wanting to take the children and staff away from the school and give them a happier perspective on the anniversary, had organised a trip to Alton Towers theme park for all those involved in the attack. I didn't want to go at all, but I knew it was going to be an exciting day out for the children and I owed it to them to be there. I had an irrational fear that we would be attacked again, simply because it was 8 July.

I felt a complete emptiness in my stomach as I arrived at the school. There were clowns smiling and dancing around, music playing, and the mayor and mayoress were there to visit the children before they went on the trip. I wanted to feel happy but I couldn't. I was met in the classroom by the excited children, all wearing the T-shirts they had been given by the police. I had mine on too; each

T-shirt read, 'St Luke's summer outing'. When the children were split into groups, I was given Maariyah, Taishion and Nakita. It was a relief not to have Francesca or Reena in my group; I would have been even more upset.

The mums were waiting outside to talk to me and hug me before we got on the coach. The press were waiting too, but I didn't want to smile for them. Yet the children were really happy, so I managed to smile too. On the coach we were given balloons, hats, cakes, drinks and biscuits, which meant even more excitement. But at Alton Towers, where even more of the media were waiting for us, I just couldn't smile. 'Come on, Lisa, give us your usual smile!' they called. I tried, but they couldn't realise how I felt behind that smile.

I felt torn apart as I watched the children enjoying the rides, eating the food provided by Alton Towers and having their faces painted. They were all laughing and enjoying their wonderful day, and I was so thankful for that. But for me so much had happened in the last year. I had lost so much, been through so much, had sixteen awards with two more to come, had felt so much physical and emotional pain, and I was about to leave these children to try and rebuild my life. I tried to tell myself that life was going to get easier, and that the last year was going to make me a better person.

Despite how I felt, the day went really well. In the middle of the afternoon, the children went to watch the *Beatrix Potter on Ice* show, while I sat outside by myself. I wanted to be left alone for a few minutes to remember. As I sat there in the sun, I began to cry, then couldn't stop. All I could think of was the children and their scars. If only I'd been a few seconds quicker. Sarah Poole came out to chat to me; she was so understanding and gave me time to get it out of my system. By the time we left Alton

Towers, I felt I had left a load of pressure and bad feeling behind me.

All the children hugged me as they got off the coach at St Luke's and went home. They were all given teddies wearing the same T-shirt as they had, reading 'St Luke's summer outing'. I made a point of speaking to Francesca's grandma and the rest of the parents; it must have been a sad day for them too. After they'd all left, I sat on the school step, thinking about the day of the attack in such detail. I found myself starting to relive the whole thing, so I quickly stood up and shook myself. In that second I thought, 'Lisa, think positive.' And things did seem to get a little better after that day. It was the end of the first year: I'd had my first Christmas since the attack, my first birthday since the attack, and now I'd lived through the first anniversary. The next year couldn't be so bad.

My positive feelings were given a knock almost straight away. The police had invited Denise and me back to their headquarters for a drink, and one of them asked if I'd seen the front of the *Express & Star*. I expected to see something about the anniversary of the attack, but instead the headline was a quote from someone at the education department saying, 'A blessing when Lisa leaves the school'. I just could not take it in. What had I done wrong? I hadn't meant to hurt anyone. The article said that because of all the publicity I was getting, the children would only be able to get back to normal after I'd left. But I never asked for all the publicity. I never phoned the papers and invited them to come and take pictures of me. In fact I was embarrassed to be in the paper so often. I couldn't help being given awards; I couldn't help it that every time I did something for charity there were photographers there. I was terribly upset that night, but the following day I had a call from the education department to say that the whole piece had been taken out of context and they were sorry. The paper rang to apologise too. I tried to let the whole situation go over my head, but I couldn't help beginning to believe that it would be better for everyone if I left. Denise tried to reassure me that I shouldn't think like that, and that I would be missed dearly by everyone. Her words helped, but the doubts remained.

Someone had bought me flowers which Mum had arranged beautifully for me, but as soon as I walked into the room I began to have terrible flashbacks. The smell was exactly the same as when I was in hospital the year before. In a wave of panic and frustration, I grabbed the flowers and threw them in the dustbin. Mum was upset, and started to talk about the waste of money and the effort that someone had put in to buying and delivering them to me. All I knew was that I had to get rid of that smell so the bad feelings would leave me.

But there were only two weeks to go until I left school, so I couldn't let the *Express & Star* story get me down too much. I had to enjoy the little time I had left with the children, as well as fit in all my other commitments. One of the most enjoyable of those commitments was an invitation to Ten Downing Street; only, last time I'd been there it was to visit John and Norma Major, whereas this time the invitation was from Tony and Cherie Blair. As part of the *Daily Star* award, St Luke's had been given £10,000, which was to be used for new playground equipment. With Denise, Pam Shee and the three children, I was to collect the cheque from Cherie Blair, but before that the *Daily Star* took us to the London Aquarium and out for lunch. The children were allowed to knock on the door at Downing Street, and were given jam sandwiches for tea and a cuddle by Tony Blair.

It was a lovely day, and so was a Buckingham Palace

garden party a few days later. One of Prince Charles's men came to talk to Mum and me as we lined up in the sunshine. He said he'd been flicking through the latest *Hello* magazine that morning and had seen the article about me, and the photographs of our house. He said to Mum, 'I must say, Mrs Potts, you have a lovely country kitchen.' After he'd gone Mum burst out, 'Country kitchen? Our blummin' dining table at the back of our normal terraced house!' But we managed to stop giggling when he came back to say Prince Charles would like to meet us. We walked down the whole line of people, and Mum was so nervous. 'Oh Lisa, I'm going to collapse!' she said as she tried to keep up. Prince Charles spoke to us for a couple of minutes, then Mum and I ate far too many of the tiny sandwiches and cakes. All the time I was aware of the fact that in another few months I'd be at the Palace again, this time to receive the George Medal.

Once the anniversary of the attack was over, I knew I had to face only one more awful day – the day of leaving school. I had been dreading it and, when the morning arrived, I didn't even want to get out of bed. I hadn't slept well again, and when I had slept I'd had awful nightmares. I wanted to hide under the quilt all day and pretend all this wasn't really happening. I was physically sick when I started to think about how much I'd miss the children. Was I doing the right thing? Everyone would think I was a coward for leaving. Should I stay after all? But no, I couldn't go on as I was. I was still sleeping badly, I couldn't focus properly, my nightmares and flashbacks continued, and I was getting my own personal life and relationships in a mess because of school. I had to admit that going into school scared me. I had gone back and faced my fears, and if things had got better as time went on, I would have stayed. But they hadn't – they'd got worse.

Denise had asked me to go to school at lunchtime, and I knew there would be some sort of farewell celebration, but I didn't know what it would be. I felt so alone and sad at home that morning. What was I going to do next? Where was I going? I knew that since the attack I had found some new skills; I had learned to communicate with people, to comfort people who had problems of their own, and to talk in front of the camera. Maybe these were even skills that had begun at school and dancing – now perhaps I could use them in a new career. But I had been so happy and content with my life as a nursery nurse. Someone once told me I would find it so hard when I stopped being famous, and that upset me. I hadn't asked for all the fame and glory, I'd just wanted to get on with being a nursery nurse. Since I was thirteen, all I'd wanted to do was look after children. Nothing else gave me more pleasure. Now I had to believe that there was something else for me in the future, however long it took to find what it was.

As I got out of my car at the school gates I knew I was going to cry. I didn't think I could go through with it. Even if I appeared happy on the outside, I was being crushed inside. I looked up at St Luke's. This was the place I had loved, and I was leaving it. I used to feel so happy to wake up in the morning and come here, to see all those lovely smiling faces laughing and calling my name. Again and again I had to tell myself it was right for me to leave. As I walked to the main entrance I glanced at the nursery doors and saw myself quite clearly running through them with children in my arms, and I heard parents screaming my name. I saw Reena with a deep cut across her face, and I felt the terrible fear that not all the children were going to survive. Then I came back to the present: it was a year later, and I was walking in to the school for my last day.

The terrifying flashback made me realise I had done my best in even going back to work in the first place. But I also felt destroyed inside to realise that of all the things that had been ripped away from me, the worst pain was having to leave the school I'd loved.

It took me a long time to get through the door of the school that day, but as soon as I opened it everything was normal. One of the children saw me, grinned cheekily and said, 'Hello Lisa Potts'. Normally I would have reminded him that my name was Miss Potts, but this was my last day, and I thought, 'If that's the way they remember me, fair enough.' Pam Shee called as usual from the office, 'Lisa, you've got loads of post in here.' I looked through the window into the dining room and saw Francesca and the rest of the children who had seen the attack. That was when I broke down. The tears rolled down my face as I thought I just could not leave these children. People had told me I must think of myself now, but it was difficult to do that when I'd formed such a bond with the children. And I think they had with me too. If any of them wanted to talk about the attack they'd just come up to me out of the blue and say, 'I saw the knife, Miss Potts,' or, 'I saw your arm, Miss Potts, and there was blood everywhere.' I would never forget the day when Reena said, 'You carried me and your arm was bleeding such a lot.' If they wanted to talk about the attack, I was there for them. I had felt they needed me during the months I was back at school. I was going to miss the children, the parents, the staff, the nursery that I'd helped set up. I so much wanted it to go back to being how it was. Nothing was the same, and there was nothing I could do about it.

I managed to stop the tears, and as I walked through the doors of the dining room all I could hear was 'Miss Potts!' 'Lisa Potts!' 'Miss, are you leaving today?' 'Miss, I've bought you a card.' 'Miss Potts, I've brought you flowers.' I wanted to turn and run; run and run until everything was all right again. But I didn't, I put on the bravest smile and went up to hug and chat to the children. Nakita, looking up at me with her beautiful eyes, asked, 'Miss Potts, why are you leaving?' What could I say? How about: 'Oh, I'm a coward and I've had enough and every night I don't sleep for fear of coming to school in case I have a flashback'? But I looked at her and said, 'Nakita, Miss Potts is leaving because she's got to find a new job.' Then Shanice climbed onto my lap and said, 'Miss Potts, I love you and I don't want you to go.' The tears were building up again. I said to the children, 'I'll see you all later; I love you all lots and lots.'

I went to the office to speak to Pam, who must have seen how I felt because she put her arm round me and asked if I was all right. I said I would be once I'd got through today. Then on to the staff-room where all the staff were assembled – even Kath who had retired by then, and Nicola who had moved on to a school nearer to her new house. It helped to know that other people had moved on too, especially Nicola, who was the closest to me. Linda had come in for the afternoon, as well as some of the part-time staff. They had put on a lovely buffet for me, and for a while it felt like it used to before. I looked out of the window at the nursery playground, this time not seeing the horror, but remembering how happy the children had been, playing so innocently at the teddy bears' picnic.

After lunch I was told we were going into the hall for a small assembly. When I walked in I saw not only the whole school and staff, but all the parents sitting there, looking at me. I couldn't believe that the parents had all turned out to see me. I sat down next to the nursery nurse who was doing my old job and said, 'I'm going to cry in a minute – help me!' She said, 'Everyone is, so I shouldn't worry.' Denise started to speak. She said it was a very sad day because Miss Potts was leaving, but it was also a time to be happy. I turned and saw the children's little faces staring up at me. 'Miss Potts is leaving' – the words kept ringing in my ears. I wasn't going to be Miss Potts to them any more. They started to sing one of my favourite songs: 'You're special, I'm special, we're special don't you see; each of us is special to God, that's the way it's meant to be; Black or white, rich or poor, each of us, God loves us all.' All those children were so special to me, and three of them in particular, because they had nearly died.

Denise called me up to the front. I thought I was going to fall over when I stood up, but I didn't. I don't remember all that Denise said about me, but I know she said I'd be greatly missed. I fought back the tears as I opened my present from the staff; a £75 Harrods gift token which they had wrapped up in gold paper with a tag saying 'Here's a little something for you to spend'. They had also bought me stamps and writing paper – the post I received and the letters I wrote had become a standing joke. There was a gift from the parents too: a suitcase to match the luggage that Dorothy Clulow had bought for my twenty-first birthday. I opened all the cards, presents and chocolates that the children had given me. Then came the most emotional time of my life. Reena and Francesca walked towards me with a huge bouquet of flowers, and in Francesca's hand was something I will always treasure. It was a wall hanging which Francesca's grandma had made for me, and as I read the words, tears started to pour silently down my face.

To Miss Potts,
My family and I are very sad to know that you are
leaving.
You do not know how much we appreciate you.
If it was not for you my granddaughter would have died.
We will always remember you in our prayers.
You have given us joy, you have given us Francesca,
If it was not for you what would we do?
Take the name of Jesus with you,
Man of sorrow and of woe,
He will give you joy and comfort,
Take it everywhere you go.
God bless and keep you.
We love you and will miss you.

I looked down and saw Francesca and Reena gazing up at me. I put out my arms and they ran into them and hugged me so tight. Those two children and Ahmed meant the world to me. The pain they had suffered was unbelievable and the pain I had suffered seemed nothing at that point. The things I had been through over that year were nothing – the flashbacks, nightmares, the new relationships I'd started to build and had lost, the sleepless nights, the worry. It all meant nothing compared to the lives of those three precious children who were still here and were still able to hug me. Children who might have been dead, but who would now grow up and perhaps have children of their own. I looked down at Francesca and Reena, then looked out to find Ahmed. I looked at the children's families and saw tears rolling down their faces too.

After the assembly there were more hugs, more cards, photos to be taken, and everyone wanting to talk to me at the same time. All the children were hugging me in turn saying, 'We love you, Miss Potts.' 'Will we see you on

TV?' 'Will we see you in the paper?' I certainly hoped they wouldn't, especially not on the news or constantly in the local paper, as I had been for the past year. I could see the families of Francesca, Reena and Ahmed were waiting to speak to me, so I went over and hugged them all. Francesca's grandma said to me, 'Thank you for every-thing, Lisa. Now you go and enjoy all the good things that are ahead of you.' And what was ahead of me, I wondered. The question ran through my head, but I wasn't going to worry about it just then.

The parents and children had said goodbye and were gone, and the teachers were clearing up in their classrooms, but I wanted to stay in the hall for a while, looking at all my cards and presents, and quietly thinking. I knew I would never forget the school, the bad times and the many good times, but now I knew I had to move on. I had to look forward, to rebuild my life. I had to learn to heal; to find the real me again; to rediscover all those feelings I'd lost. There were many more tears as I gathered up my things, packed them into the car and said my last goodbyes. I hugged Denise and Pam, and said goodbye to them. But turning for one final look at St Luke's before I drove away, I smiled. And no smile is so beautiful as the one that has struggled through pain.

Afterword

Of course, that wasn't the last time I went back to St Luke's, and neither did my life suddenly change dramatically. It's been a slow process.

The first six weeks away from school were wonderful. I didn't miss the children dreadfully to start with because I felt as if I was having the six weeks' holiday like everybody else. I had time to think and time to heal in those weeks. I went to Brownie camp and the Church Pastoral Aid Society camp, as I did every year, and had a wonderful time. I spent some time in London, and a day which will always stay in my memory is when I went to Harrods to spend the token the staff had given me as a leaving present. I looked up and saw Princess Diana standing next to me. She caught my eye and said, 'Hello, how are you feeling now?' I thanked her and said I was very well, and she gave me the most beautiful smile and said, 'I'm so glad, Lisa.' It wasn't until later that it sunk in that she really did know who I was, even though she met so many new people every day.

Three weeks later I was at Brownie camp when one of the leaders came in and told us that Princess Diana had died in a car crash. Like the rest of the world I couldn't take it in. She was such a beautiful, caring and compassionate person. I was very fortunate to have met her. A couple of days later, after I'd been to the Grosvenor Hotel to present a television award, I went up to Kensington Palace. The flowers had only just begun to form a carpet, and I stood there in the absolute silence of the early morning, surrounded by hundreds of people. I laid a candle and photograph of Diana among the other tributes.

The next day I was off to America again, this time with my friend Danielle, for the holiday awarded to me by Virgin Holidays. It was another opportunity to rest, think and allow myself to heal. It wasn't until I came back from holiday that it really hit me – I had left my job and I wasn't a nursery nurse any more. I missed work so much and longed to go in to visit, but I thought it was best if I stayed away for a while. However, I only managed two days at home before I went in to see the children – I just couldn't keep away any longer!

Life was much quieter, and I had time to reply to some more of the letters from the pile which didn't seem to get smaller. I began to sort out where I was going and what my priorities were. I was receiving £80 a week industrial benefit, but I was in demand from all sorts of people so I decided to become self-employed and find a way of supporting myself. I found an agent, who began to get work for me that was unconnected with the attack. I know that people's interest in me stemmed from the attack – that's how they'd first heard of me – but there was no need for me to go on talking about it now. I was given different TV projects, and became a local radio presenter for a week, as holiday cover for the regular presenter. I enjoy working on TV and radio as I get to meet all sorts of people and the work I do is very varied. I've also discovered the ability to listen to people as they talk about the things they've suffered. My prayer book, *Thank You, God*, was published at the beginning of November and I travelled around even more to do book signings. I didn't think anyone would come to them, but they did.

I began to do more regular charity work too. Sometimes I'd open a charity shop, or give after-dinner speeches at fund-raising evenings. I took on charity events of all sorts, for many different charities, although time didn't permit me to do all I was offered.

My appointments to sort out my compensation award didn't stop. My local education department paid me £3,750, but the full award is still being dealt with by the Criminal Injuries Board. Neither did the appointments at the hospital stop. I still have to go for regular occupational therapy, and I'll almost definitely have to go through another operation. I still have pain in my left arm and there is limited movement and little feeling around the scarred area. When it's very cold I have great difficulty in bending it and gripping. I still get many headaches and on bad days I black out. But I don't usually let any of it get me down.

The awards didn't stop either. I was named as one of the three Champions of Courage, along with Rita Restorick, whose son was killed by the IRA, and Doreen Lawrence, whose son was killed in a racist attack. We were given our awards by Queen Noor of Jordan at the Women of the Year lunch at the Savoy. But at these ceremonies it wasn't always me who was receiving awards. I began to be invited back to the ceremonies where I'd been given awards the year before, so that I could give out the awards myself. At the Midland Diamond Awards I still cried for every award-winner, and I told them I was the worst person to give an award because I couldn't keep my eyes dry. It was so special to give my Super Diamond Award back, and present it to Shaun Cooke, a brave little four-year-old who was born with his heart on the wrong side and who suffered from a rare cancer. His doctors described him as an inspiration. I was overwhelmed when he insisted on leaving his wheelchair behind and, with a huge effort, walked on to the stage. When he reached me I took him in my arms and wept.

I presented the Duke of Edinburgh Awards at St James's Palace and, of course, met the Duke himself. And then it was November, and time to receive the George Medal from the Queen. I felt so happy as I waited in line to be presented and to receive the medal. My life was no longer about the machete attack heroine, but about Lisa Potts who had moved forward and started to heal. I felt honoured and delighted to be standing next to Paul Burrell, Princess Diana's butler. I was so touched when he said that of all the people he could have been standing next to, I was the one that Princess Diana would have chosen. At the far end of the room I could see Mum, Dad and Lee watching the Queen presenting medals to all those ahead of me. I tried to take in every second of this stunning experience, as the line moved forward.

It was almost my turn. I said a quick prayer, then walked forward and curtsied in front of the Queen. She presented me with the medal, saying it was for 'absolute bravery'. I said, 'Thank you your Majesty, but it was purely instinctive.' She asked how the children were coping, and whether my injuries were healing. I showed her my arm and told her I was doing very well. She smiled, put out her hand and I lightly shook it. I stepped backwards, curtsied again, smiled and walked away. Afterwards the press seemed to concentrate on Paul Burrell and me, and we gave one interview after another.

The day didn't end there, there was more to come. On the train going back to Wolverhampton everyone was congratulating me and asking to see my medal, and Virgin Trains presented me with a bottle of champagne. At home

I changed, then drove off to Birmingham, where Philippa Parlor and I were to receive the West Midlands Police Authority's Good Citizenship Commendation. I was thrilled that my 'little sister', Clare, was coming with me to receive my eighteenth award. It was good to go back to the Midlands for my last award, because after all that was where it all happened.

Through all this time, I could feel that my healing was taking place. I was meeting Phil for counselling once a week instead of once a fortnight, which helped so much now that I had time really to think about what we'd discussed. I also started some private counselling in Birmingham. I began a new relationship, too, which felt good for me because I knew my life was starting to sort itself out. And, of course, I started to write this book. I believe this has been a major part of my healing process. It's as if I've left a lot of the flashbacks behind in the book. My flashbacks come much less often now – just occasionally if something happens which reminds me of the attack. I've learnt to stop and tell myself it isn't really happening and it will soon pass. I still have the occasional nightmare, but nothing compared to how it was at school. I've also sorted out my feelings of guilt – I've learnt to no longer blame myself as I realise I did as much as I could on that day.

I look back on the past year and wonder if I am no longer the person I was before the day of the attack. Maybe I have developed more skills, confidence and knowledge in some areas which have enabled me to start work in new fields. Whatever happens in my life and career, I am thankful that I have the character I have today, which enables me to try to put the past behind me.

I cannot thank my wonderful and supportive family enough, who never let me down, even through the darkest times. Thank you so much to Pam and Hazel, for all the support they gave to me and my family. I certainly could never have been the person I am today without you all. Neither could I have got through without the massive support of my closest friends: Clare, for helping me in and out of all the baths; Marc, for all his love and support which will never be forgotten; both Nicis, for listening to me going on and on and on; Dawn, for letting me share the miracle of birth and for all her wonderful advice. Thank you to the rest of my family and friends – I'm sorry I can't mention you all personally.

I want to say a huge thank you to the staff at St Luke's for putting up with me, and special love to all the St Luke's children and their parents; thanks to the medical staff at New Cross Hospital, the police and ambulance staff who looked after me – without their quick and professional actions, who knows where I would be today?; and thanks to Phil Smith for giving up his time to help me through my flashbacks, and to Peter Wilson and Larry Warr for all the fun I had while filming.

Thank you to Judith Longman for all her support and encouragement during the writing of this book; thank you to Peter for the wonderful ideas and for the title of the book, and for all the support and encouragement he has given me over the past year; and a massive thank you to Jill Worth, because without her this book wouldn't have been possible.

I would like to thank the people of the country for all their support which certainly restored my faith in humanity. And finally – thank you, God.